Cover Image Credit/Copyright Attribution: IIIerlok_Xolms/Shutterstock

SSR Paper 14

DDR and SSR in War-to-Peace Transition

Christopher von Dyck

Published by
Ubiquity Press Ltd.
6 Osborn Street, Unit 2N
London E1 6TD

First published 2016
Transferred to Ubiquity Press 2018

Editors: Heiner Hänggi & Albrecht Schnabel
Associate editor: Fairlie Chappuis
Editorial assistance: Kathrin Reed
Copy editor: Cherry Ekins

DOI: https://doi.org/10.5334/bby

This book was originally published by the Geneva Centre for the Democratic Control of Armed Forces (DCAF), an international foundation whose mission is to assist the international community in pursuing good governance and reform of the security sector. The title transferred to Ubiquity Press when the series moved to an open access platform. The full text of this book was peer reviewed according to the original publisher's policy at the time. The original ISBN for this title was 978-92-9222-412-7.

SSR Papers is a flagship DCAF publication series intended to contribute innovative thinking on important themes and approaches relating to security sector reform (SSR) in the broader context of security sector governance (SSG). Papers provide original and provocative analysis on topics that are directly linked to the challenges of a governance-driven security sector reform agenda. SSR Papers are intended for researchers, policy-makers and practitioners involved in this field.

The views expressed are those of the author(s) alone and do not in any way reflect the views of the institutions referred to or represented within this paper.

Suggested citation:
von Dyck, C. 2018. *DDR and SSR in War-to-Peace Transition*. London: Ubiquity Press. DOI: https://doi.org/10.5334/bby. License: CC-BY 4.0

Contents

Introduction

Disarmament, demobilization and reintegration (DDR) and security sector reform (SSR) have become integral components in the international community's peacebuilding toolkit for countries recovering from internal conflict.[1] In recent years the United Nations (UN) and Organisation for Economic Co-operation and Development (OECD) nations have called for more closely coordinated DDR and SSR strategies in their peacekeeping and statebuilding interventions, and emphasized the need for better planning, implementation and monitoring frameworks to make them more effective on the ground.[2] Academic and policy research has also suggested that DDR and SSR programmes could be more closely linked,[3] although some practitioners cast doubt about the feasibility of operationalizing a policy "link" in practice.[4]

Debates on whether and how DDR and SSR could be effectively linked have so far been theoretical and normative in nature. The existing literature lacks sufficient empirical data taking into account the transitional context in which these processes take place. Policy-oriented research on DDR and SSR tends to prioritize supply-side considerations related to coordination, financing and programming.[5] Less attention has been focused on demand-side considerations related to how DDR and SSR interact in local political and state formation processes after war. The main aim of this paper is thus to provide an empirical understanding of how SSR and DDR were linked in two past peacebuilding interventions in West Africa in order to identify opportunities and constraints for establishing closer practical linkages in war-to-peace transitions.

The space in which countries transition from war to peace involves complicated political processes shaped by ongoing conflicts and the negotiation and distribution of political (and economic) power, especially for control of state power. Countries in transition from intrastate warfare often lack an effective state capable of enforcing contracts or political commitments between factions. In this institutional vacuum, conflict is often resolved outside formal and institutionalized political structures. DDR and SSR interventions must be understood within this context of formal and informal negotiation processes. DDR and SSR programmes have been largely shaped by external actors seeking agreement between powerful factions at the negotiation table. However, a significant gap exists between the formal terms of an agreement and the operationalization of those terms. The terms for DDR and SSR tend to be standardized according to international norms, but the implementation phase is far from an exact science. Formal and informal agreements on the terms for DDR and SSR are often purposively vague and designed to be sorted out later depending on local conditions and the emergent nature of relations over how power vacuums are to be settled.[6]

This paper assumes that in transitional statebuilding processes[7] there may be incentives for central rulers to adopt (or at least seem to embrace) certain elements of DDR and/or SSR when these allow them to consolidate their domestic power[8] and/or enhance their legitimacy internationally.[9] DDR may influence a political process that entails shifting the balance of power from irregular factions to a recognized central state capable of establishing (and maintaining) itself as the sole political authority with the legitimacy to use force. SSR seeks to build on the gains from this shift to enhance state capacity to provide security and legitimize state rule through democratic governance, particularly the democratic civilian control of the security sector, within a larger framework of the rule of law and respect for human rights. From this perspective, this paper argues that DDR and SSR can be characterized as distinct processes with overlapping objectives on a war–peace transition spectrum seeking to restore a central state authority and reduce the power of irregular armed factions.

To understand how DDR and SSR interact within the political context of a transitional setting, this paper argues that it helps to consider how local political processes place constraints on the implementation of peacebuilding interventions.[10] More integrated DDR–SSR strategies are likely to fail if the intervention's logic is based on a flawed analysis of local political conditions and processes. This paper identifies four dimensions critical for post-conflict political environments in statebuilding literature, which together constitute broad parameters for taking into account how politics in a post-civil-war transition might condition or constrain opportunities for DDR–SSR synergies:

1. The nature of the conflict, how the war ends and how this shapes the balance of forces between the warring factions (political settlement).
2. The nature and interests of central state authority (balance of forces within the ruling coalition).
3. The central state's relative strength *vis-à-vis* the relative influence of international actors.
4. Local capacities for change.

To test these ideas, this paper comparatively explores two West African DDR and SSR experiences. The central research questions addressed here are what role did DDR and SSR play in the local context, what was the nature of the respective DDR and SSR interventions and to what extent was a link established between DDR and SSR interventions in practice? The case studies focus on Sierra Leone and Liberia for several reasons. First, these two countries hosted extensive international DDR and SSR programmes at different times during the early 2000s as part of the global community's response to ending civil conflicts and (re)building state institutions in the aftermath of war. Sierra Leone, and to a lesser extent Liberia, became an important testing ground for experimenting with and developing concurrent DDR–SSR interventions. Both cases feature a prominent role for DDR and SSR in the broader process of restoring central states that had essentially fragmented and collapsed.[11] They involved different Western (UK and US) and/or regional powers serving in coordination and leadership roles at different points of time in support of SSR, making it possible to disaggregate and analyse the various roles that external donors assume and discern their actual and potential influence over policy-making and in altering power relations.

While the Sierra Leonean and Liberian post-conflict contexts can be described as "relatively benign" cases of post-war peacebuilding compared to Afghanistan or Iraq, due to the relatively minor geopolitical significance of these countries,[12] they can tell us about how British and US-led post-conflict interventions engage in "second-order" countries. This is an important starting point to take stock of the relationship between DDR and SSR in the context of wider post-conflict statebuilding processes. Additionally, while the West African cases may be considered first-generation SSR programmes, the lessons from these interventions have yet to be extracted systematically. Despite the fact that this paper only focuses on two states, the analysis of these comparatively older and presumably more benign cases is empirically valuable from both academic and practical perspectives.

It is necessary to take into account the fact that the transition path adopted by these two cases was quite different. In Sierra Leone the main anti-government warring faction (the Revolutionary United Front) was defeated at the end of the war. In Liberia three irregular armed factions became the state through a negotiated political settlement that was implemented by international donors. These cases demonstrate how variations in underlying political settlements – i.e. their nature and relative degree of stability – can lead to different outcomes during DDR–SSR processes. There were a number of facilitating conditions that aided the DDR and SSR processes in both countries. Sierra Leone and Liberia did not experience a resumption in fighting after their political settlements were established in May 2001 and August 2003 respectively, but for different reasons. War fatigue was certainly omnipresent in both countries at the end of their wars. Robust UN interventions (led by large UN peacekeeping missions) and direct Western diplomatic, development and military support, along with regional commitment (from Nigeria), effectively shored up the existing political settlements and, to a large extent, sent strong signals to all parties that a negotiated peace was possible.

The rest of this paper is structured as follows. Next, a review of the emerging discourse and underlying ideas and assumptions of DDR and SSR is presented, with a discussion of recent claims about an emerging DDR–SSR nexus in some peacebuilding policy circles. This section also examines the relationship between DDR and SSR in the context of war-to-peace transitions. The discussion is then brought into focus through an examination of DDR and SSR practices in Sierra Leone (2001–2004) and Liberia (2003–2005). The conclusion summarizes the empirical evidence and considers how the DDR–SSR relationship can be enhanced in war-to-peace transition contexts.

The DDR–SSR Nexus

This section reviews the emerging discourse and underlying ideas and assumptions embedded in DDR and SSR. DDR and SSR engagements are respectively disaggregated to demonstrate a better understanding of their broader relationship with the state restoration and building processes. This informs the discussion on the nexus between DDR and SSR, followed by presentation of the relationship between DDR and SSR in the context of war-to-peace transitions.

DDR: Origins, evolution and discourse

The evolution of DDR programmes[13] is linked directly to the broad policy setting in which early post-Cold War UN peacekeeping missions were implemented during the 1990s and early 2000s. DDR interventions have received considerable attention in the UN system in the context of efforts to improve peacekeeping strategies and consider possible UN system-wide structural reforms since the late 1990s.

DDR is a broad label for a cluster of interventions to disarm, demobilize and reintegrate members of warring factions and antagonistic groups once a conflict has ended. The aim of UN DDR programmes is to remove "the immediate threat to a fragile peace posed by groups of armed, uncontrolled and unemployed ex-combatants".[14] DDR programmes are usually implemented under short timeframes (one to three years) during the "emergency phase" of a transition when immediate results are needed.[15]

The UN defines disarmament as "the collection, documentation, control and disposal of small arms, ammunition, explosives and light and heavy weapons of combatants and often also of the civilian population. Disarmament also includes the development of responsible arms management programmes."[16] Many experts prioritize this component of DDR over the other two.

According to the UN, demobilization involves the formal and controlled processing of individual combatants and cantoning them in designated areas.[17] This often involves UN military forces due to the focus on technical military duties, such as monitoring compliance. Demobilization usually extends to what the UN calls "reinsertion": short-term transitional assistance for ex-combatants to help them cover their immediate material needs before their reintegration into civilian life.

Reintegration can be considered as a starting point for offering alternative livelihoods to recently disarmed combatants or as a motivator for them to leave their irregular factions.[18] The UN defines "reintegration" as "part of the general development of a country and a *national responsibility*",[19] considering it as a long-term "process by which ex-combatants acquire civilian status and gain sustainable employment and income".[20] However, there is a strong economic and programmatic bias in the delivery of reintegration assistance. Reintegration emphasizes the transfer of skills through vocational training and education to transform individual ex-combatants into productive members of society.[21] While there is wide recognition that reintegration is a long-term process, the programmatic assistance (in the form of scholarships or skills training) is usually offered for only a few years.

Learning from the DDR experiments of UN missions in Sierra Leone, Liberia and the Democratic Republic of the Congo, among others, the UN has enhanced its experience and knowledge in DDR. DDR programmes are now a systematic part of most UN-mandated peacekeeping missions. Several international initiatives have been organized since 2004 to codify norms and standards for UN DDR activities. Beginning in March 2005, the UN's Inter-Agency Working Group on DDR (IAWG-DDR) brought together practitioners, policy-makers, donors and research communities to take stock of and extract lessons learned from past UN DDR practice. However, the resulting 2006 policy document[22] provided no clear understanding of how DDR relates to wider state restoration and power consolidation efforts in recipient countries.

DDR is a highly contested activity, and its definition, scope and objectives are the subject of intense debate among scholars and UN practitioners. There is no consensus on whether it should be conceived as a short-term tool focused on security and stability or a potential bridge to longer-term development (hence stronger emphasis on reintegration). DDR programmes in their short timeframes tend to focus on the need to "stabilize" the political context in favour of a central state, potentially leading to broader state consolidation. Some observers (the "minimalists") argue that DDR is and should remain a tool to reduce the number of weapons in circulation in a society, with a view to stabilizing the country and reducing the risk of renewed violence in the short term to allow other aspects of peacebuilding to take root.[23] This minimalist approach is sometimes called quick-impact stabilization, which is informed by problem-solving assumptions.[24] Others (the "maximalists") believe that DDR can be a potential bridge to development if broader and more long-term conceptualizations can be operationalized.[25] The recent UN DDR discourse often mentions a multidimensional nature, involving political, social and economic activities taking place within "a process that contributes to security and stability in the post-conflict recovery context".[26] The central problem with both minimalist and maximalist concepts of DDR is the absence of any explicit discussion about the relationship between DDR and struggles over state power. There is a tendency to assume that DDR programmes have little to do with emergent processes of contestation for power between different warring factions. Therefore, these perspectives have simply taken for granted that UN DDR interventions have nothing to do with state restoration and the host state's consolidation of power, when, in reality, these political processes cannot be separated from DDR interventions.

SSR: Origins, evolution and discourse

SSR emerged as a new area of security and development assistance in the late 1990s and has gained increased recognition as an important element of international support in transitional societies. The early SSR agenda sought to conceptualize policies of reform for security forces based on experiences from Central and Eastern European states at the end of the Cold War.[27] Over the past few years more attention has focused on understanding how SSR interventions are related to DDR, and how its tasks can contribute to building capacity *within* states to deliver security and justice for that state and its people.[28]

The SSR agenda acknowledges that – as former UN Secretary-General Kofi Annan noted – the security sector should "be subject to the same standards of efficiency, equity and accountability as any other [public] service".[29] SSR policy-makers and practitioners tend to focus on three short- to long-term tasks. The first is to restore order by neutralizing and delegitimizing so-called illegal, non-statutory armed groups (militias, gangs, community defence groups, etc.). The second task involves re-establishing formal state security forces to maintain public order within the rule of law. However, this paper argues that this perspective presumes the existence of a formal state and takes for granted certain key processes involved in restoring the central state and its consolidation. The third task involves restoring or establishing state institutions that oversee and monitor these security forces to ensure compliance with formal rules and norms. These include but are not limited to executive actors such as the interior and defence ministries, parliamentary bodies, the judicial system and civil society.[30] This is further complicated in contexts where the democratic political control of armed and other security forces has not yet been institutionalized.

Thus, according to Hendrickson and Karkoszka, the institutional framework for managing the security sector needs to be strengthened through three steps related to democratic governance: ensuring the proper location of security activities within a constitutional framework and developing security policies and instruments to implement them; building the capacity of policy-makers to assess the nature of security threats effectively and design strategic responses supportive of wider development goals; and strengthening accountability mechanisms for the security forces by making state and non-state actors legally responsible for monitoring security policy and enforcing the constitution and law fulfil their functions effectively.[31]

The first decade of SSR interventions focused on bilateral efforts, which aimed to alter the rules and norms *within* developing countries' security sectors to enhance state capacity building, promote good governance and enhance the delivery of basic human security. Various OECD deliberations and statements during the early to mid-2000s shaped this bilateral agenda, which sought to shape preferences of actors in the security sector and alter norms, practices and incentives within states in the developing world by attempting to inculcate good principles of accountability, transparency and participatory decision-making into security institutions.[32] Such reforms during war–peace transitions require considerable financial commitment and significant external involvement – a process fraught with many complicated challenges.

Today the UN and other regional and multilateral organizations (the African Union, the Economic Community of West African States (ECOWAS), the European Union, NATO, the Organization for Security and Co-operation in Europe) have become much more actively involved in supporting SSR programmes in member and partner countries. In an effort to address some of the tensions over international versus locally driven SSR, the 2007 OECD-DAC (OECD Development Assistance Committee) *Handbook on Security System Reform* stressed the importance of enhancing security sector governance[33] within a framework that supports local ownership.[34] On the issue of local ownership, the handbook emphasizes the need to foster a supportive political environment through in-depth knowledge of a given reform context. This is considered essential to the assessment and design of SSR programmes so international actors avoid exacerbating endogenous considerations or social cleavages. It is worth noting that the OECD-DAC handbook offers no practical guidance on DDR–SSR linkages, but simply states that DDR and SSR are "often best considered together as part of a comprehensive security and justice development programme".[35]

Over the past few years multilateral actors have developed elaborate policy and operational frameworks on SSR. UN Security Council members have been actively involved in supporting SSR programmes and ensuring greater clarity on how the organization can engage in SSR-related activities in the spirit of the UN Charter. The 2008 UN Secretary-General's report on "Securing peace and development: The role of the United Nations in supporting security sector reform" was a landmark statement on how relevant UN bodies and agencies can support SSR activities.[36] It set the "gold standard" for UN support in the area of SSR in the context of UN peacebuilding missions, defining it as a

> process of assessment, review and implementation as well as monitoring and evaluation *led by national authorities* that has as its goal the enhancement of effective and accountable security for the state and its peoples without discrimination and with full respect of human rights and the rule of law.[37]

One of the crucial conclusions that can be derived from UN policy statements is the avoidance by UN bodies of being seen as engaging in domestic statebuilding tasks on behalf of member states. Similar to its DDR practice, the UN's structural and political characteristics constrain the degree of involvement and the methods that UN field-level SSR practitioners can employ.[38] The UN Security Council stresses that the UN has a "crucial role to play in promoting comprehensive, coherent, and coordinated international support to nationally owned security sector reform programmes, implemented with the consent of the countries concerned".[39]

Some Western scholars have criticized the SSR agenda for being idealistic and even arrogant in assuming that outside actors can build states in non-Western societies – a critique which would apply to all statebuilding activities.[40] Governments in the South – albeit those which have not been involved in SSR programmes – have criticized SSR as a form of Western interventionism in their internal affairs.[41] SSR practices are meant to be fundamentally distinct from Cold War security assistance, given the concept's normative emphasis on democratic governance as a core and explicit statebuilding end-goal. This core principle was based on assertions about the need for states to govern their societies according to liberal, democratic principles and standards. SSR policy perspectives typically have an ideal-typical Weberian state with two pillars of statehood in mind: first, the contemporary state must establish itself as the sole political authority capable of legitimately using force; and second, the exercise of state power must be based on rationalized and routine practices in the security sector, bureaucratic profession-alism and institutionalized forms of governance, including the development and implementation of impersonal and rationally organized state security policies.[42] This link is explicitly argued in the 2005 OECD-DAC report in its statement that SSR is fundamentally concerned with "spreading Western norms and practices to inform how security institutions should be governed".[43]

To summarize, in contrast to the shorter timeframes seen with DDR, SSR policy emphasizes medium- to long-term goals related to improving institutional and governance capacity of states. SSR efforts are geared towards supporting states to achieve lasting state and human security through longer-term reform.[44] Regardless of the differences in SSR approaches and methods, they all imply that the real challenge facing reform of post-conflict states is not so much knowing where to end up (provision of security to the state and its society within a framework of democratic governance, rule of law and respect for human rights), but searching for a feasible path to get there. For Donais, the key puzzle is "how incentive structures can be changed to make SSR an attractive proposition for as many as possible".[45] But despite this growing interest in SSR as an intervention aiming to build state capacity to deliver human security within democratic frameworks, existing research has not yet identified a process for how this can be achieved, nor the causal mechanisms that influence the process. The SSR discourse seems to conflate different aspects of rebuilding states, while analytically separating this process from the highly contentious power struggles that ensue during politically charged war–peace transitions.[46] Additionally, there is no theory of change for translating broad and normative SSR principles, such as local ownership, transparency or accountability, into concrete, actionable policies.[47]

A DDR–SSR nexus?

Over the last few years, UN member states have increasingly recognized the need for closer linkages between DDR and SSR in UN peacebuilding practice.[48] Linkages have been hindered in the past for three main reasons. First, DDR and SSR agendas have evolved and operated largely independently of each other. Second, there is often little collaboration between DDR and SSR specialists, due in part to the considerable disagreement on mandates and the perceived need to avoid mission creep.[49] Third, there are multiple viewpoints on the relationship between DDR and SSR. Conceptually, some sources consider DDR as a subcomponent of the larger SSR agenda.[50] In line with the argument of this paper, others view them as "two separate but related activities".[51]

In response to an increased demand for better DDR–SSR synergies, the IAWG-DDR commissioned the Geneva Centre for the Democratic Control of Armed Forces (DCAF) in 2008 to consider how UN support to DDR and SSR processes could be more systematically linked in practice. This resulted in Module 6.10 on "Disarmament, demobilization and reintegration and security sector reform" in the updated version of the UN Integrated Disarmament, Demobilization and Reintegration Standards (IDDRS) in December 2009.[52] The module identified three practical links between DDR and SSR: linking disarmament and demobilization with national security policy; linking military and police integration with SSR; and sharing information between DDR and SSR actors for planning purposes.

While the first identified link between disarmament and demobilization and the national security policy-making component of SSR may be desirable in theory, the module problematically assumes a central state authority already consolidated and legitimate. It also takes for granted that a durable political settlement underlying state authority is in place, with sufficient harmony between the actors to develop national security policies. The reality is that most of the long-term, contentious political issues related to national security are not typically addressed until conflicts have settled down.[53] Few countries are in a position to consider national security planning during DDR programming. Thus operationalizing a link between SSR planning related to national security policy and short-term DDR is difficult to achieve in practice.

Military and police integration programmes are widely used in post-conflict settings and often involve some overlap between DDR and SSR, as suggested by the second link in the module.[54] As a substrategy of SSR, military and police integration programmes imply that post-conflict states are willing and able to integrate ex-combatants as security personnel or, less commonly, merge competing factions to create a new national army.[55] The sustainability of such programmes depends on the political settlement and existing political configuration. In particular, military reintegration programmes (MRPs) have been used as a strategy following negotiated peace settlements in approximately one-third of the world's civil wars since the 1990s.[56] They often involve a range of short-term activities to establish or reconfigure a post-conflict state's internal rules and institutions for recruitment and vetting new recruits for national security forces. MRPs have SSR-related implications for determining ranks within the armed forces in order to forge effective hierarchical command and control structures. Such measures are also needed to prevent individuals trained in violence from creating instability.[57] To link demobilization and security sector integration, it thus seems necessary to invest in an information/intelligence-gathering and data management system for demobilized personnel.

This is related to the third link identified in the module, with some sources suggesting that links should be established between DDR and SSR practitioners for the purpose of information sharing to reduce programme implementation costs. The module reinforces the importance of information sharing to support the enhancement and enforcement of good international practices on human rights and governance. It is not clear what mechanisms have been used in past interventions that can effectively enhance cooperation between civilian and security actors in this process. However, it is standard practice for UN actors to support the establishment of national DDR commissions in host countries. These national commissions typically work closely with UN DDR actors to establish a database system for demobilized combatants for the purpose of enhancing information flows for planning and monitoring DDR outcomes.[58] This information can be useful for SSR planners and practitioners to avoid false identification and prevent multiple payments to combatants.

While making the case for programmatic, thematic and technical links between DDR and SSR, the module lacks an analysis of DDR and SSR from the demand side. This leaves a gap in how their components relate to local political processes and broader statebuilding and restoration processes.[59] In general, few studies have addressed how DDR relates to statebuilding and SSR. Yet this could be a step towards overcoming the outlined challenges associated with linking DDR and SSR in practice, and an integral contribution to establishing a DDR–SSR nexus.

DDR and SSR in transitions from war to peace

This paper assumes that the relationship between DDR and SSR is poorly understood due to the unique complexities of war–peace transitions in post-civil-war contexts. A more sophisticated understanding of how DDR and SSR are related in war-to-peace transitions is required to facilitate an exploratory study of the empirical reality. This section therefore explores the question of how DDR and SSR are conceptually linked in relation to a broader state restoration process. It first disaggregates the three components of DDR to demonstrate how they relate to state restoration and may be broadly linked to SSR. Second, it provides a conceptual understanding of DDR and SSR in war–peace transitions by considering how the two processes interact in transitional political spaces, focusing on the four dimensions identified in the introduction as critical for post-conflict political environments.

Linking DDR to statebuilding
Disarmament is closely related to a state's struggle to (re-)establish a monopoly over the means of coercion. This is in turn a principal objective of SSR: ensuring that the state has a monopoly over the use of force under a democratic framework of management and oversight, accountability and the rule of law. Disarmament is furthermore closely linked to political bargaining processes that occur between state and non-state actors vying for power. Typically, a political agreement between the warring factions is a necessary but not always sufficient condition for local disarmament implementation. Similarly, the removal and subsequent disarmament of rival local armed actors can be considered as a facilitator for implementing SSR in such contexts. DDR can potentially benefit from SSR in cases where armed groups have incentives to hold on to their arms after a political solution has been reached, because SSR aims to transform the state's unstable security environment and culture of mistrust by establishing effective, representative and accountable security and justice providers and management and oversight actors.[60]

In certain contexts external actors may assume a role as a third-party peacekeeping force and must credibly commit to executing tasks related to disarmament that are normally left to a central state, including guaranteeing equitable security, enforcing sanctions through coercion and distributing incentives to compel antagonistic factions to surrender their weapons.[61] Yet DDR cannot be a replacement for local state capacity. The sustainability of disarmament also depends on the central state's capacity to maintain the balance of power, impose its will on potential rival armed groups and deliver security and public goods (i.e. protection) on an equitable basis.[62]

Supply-side UN DDR programmes seek to support UN member states to strengthen their national security. They can bestow legitimacy and recognition on certain domestic actors over others. However, UN DDR programmes are constrained by the UN Charter and the political preferences of UN Security Council member states, meaning it is critical that the government in power is internationally recognized. Since the UN Security Council rarely, if ever, authorizes forceful disarmament of armed groups, conventional DDR approaches require a political settlement first and voluntary participation by the warring factions.[63]

Demobilization is closely tied to the process of determining winners and losers in reaching a peace settlement because it can contribute to reducing further the political and military influence of irregular factions. The central state may be responsible for deciding which of its combatants will be discharged and must impose its will on the defeated groups, by for instance dismantling their command structures. In a negotiated peace, demobilization is closely connected to disarmament because commanders often maintain their networks with combatants as resources for potential remobilization.[64] In the modern era, inducements are often used to shift incentives for combatants to non-violent civilian livelihoods.

The reintegration process is also linked to statebuilding and SSR, because effective reintegration can reduce the number of ex-combatants who could mobilize autonomously in the country.[65] Success may depend on the extent to which local state representatives are involved in the local-level reintegration processes. Incentives may be used to integrate some irregular combatants into state decision-making structures or the state security apparatus.[66] In response to failed or incomplete outcomes of DDR programmes, reintegration approaches have gradually shifted from ex-combatant-centred programmes to community-driven initiatives involving, in many cases, local state officials.[67] Successful reintegration depends on supply-side factors, such as the socio-economic conditions in communities and the capacity of local labour markets to absorb ex-combatants.[68]

However, this focus on the supply-side considerations of DDR overlooks possible links with political processes that are deeply implicated in post-conflict statebuilding tasks and could also act as facilitators or spoilers for SSR. As assumed in this paper, if DDR and SSR activities in post-conflict contexts are linked to statebuilding processes, then restoring a central state as the legitimate political authority capable of wielding force is a "first-order" concern. Consequently, it is important to consider how DDR and SSR interact in transitional political spaces. As mentioned, there are currently no formal models to assess how DDR and SSR processes fit within immediate war–peace transitions.

Conditions for a DDR and SSR link

The second part of this subsection therefore seeks to develop a conceptual understanding to facilitate an exploratory study of the empirical reality in the West African case studies. Comprehending the nature of fluid domestic power relations in the process of restoring a central state and the relative influence of third-party actors is critical for linking DDR and SSR in transitional contexts. As the following comparative case studies suggest, external support to DDR and SSR alters the way these programmes are implemented and received. Peacebuilding models and the literature on DDR and SSR can be useful in calling attention to some core features that shape the local political space and capacity for peacebuilding in post-civil-war transitions.[69] Based on the existing literature, as mentioned earlier, four dimensions can be identified for shaping political settlements: the nature of power relations between the warring factions at the end of the conflict; the nature of the central state authority; the relative power of the central state *vis-à-vis* the relative influence of international actors; and local capacities for change.

The nature of the conflict and how it ends form a first crucial factor in linking DDR and SSR in war-to-peace transitions because they shape subsequent options for post-conflict peacebuilding.[70] The literature on civil wars highlights that an outright victory results in a decisive end to a war. Military victories tend to occur more frequently, with roughly three-quarters of civil wars between 1945 and 1993 ending through a decisive victory.[71] If a stalemate ensues, third-party mediators often step in to broker an agreement that divides power among some or all of the local actors.[72] Quantitative studies on civil war resolution confirm that roughly one-quarter of intrastate conflicts end through negotiated settlements.[73] In many conflicts, third-party (international) actors intervene to "stop the fighting"[74] but end up contributing to a more fragile peace.[75] These interventions can interrupt an unfinished war and produce unstable power relations between factions.[76] The outcome of these unfinished processes will depend on the warring parties' capacity to leverage their military power effectively relative to their rivals and the extent to which third parties alter local power dynamics.[77]

In a negotiated peace, forging a political settlement based on consensus between the main warring parties is a first-order concern for statebuilding and implementing disarmament.[78] Without a consensus among the parties, groups will continue to have strong incentives to hold on to their armaments and keep their forces mobilized. The nature of the conflict is important for negotiating peace, particularly if its onset is the result of deep-seated divisions between social groups over the distribution of power.[79] Different political settlements result in different incentives for DDR and SSR.

Creating a process and establishing conditions for political dialogue and negotiation require overcoming domestic security dilemmas to build confidence among the parties that their security will be guaranteed.[80] Third-party security guarantees do not ensure that parties will negotiate in good faith, but are a first step to attenuating the security dilemma. There is an important distinction between short-term security provided to leaders during the negotiating period and longer-term security to ensure that personal interests of the powerful can be realized by the terms of the peace.[81]

The onset of political bargaining represents a mere snapshot in time of a particular power configuration. Outside the institutional formalities of negotiation there are power relations on the ground, which can shift to affect the overall configuration of power between the factions during negotiation. Furthermore, mediators and the warring factions are constrained by limited and incomplete information about each other's resources, strategies and internal command structures.

The second step is to consider how a political settlement has consequences for a post-conflict state's capacity or willingness to overcome collective action problems: the nature of the central state authority.[82] After war ends, new central rulers may be compelled to engage in first-order state-making tasks, including some bargaining with societal groups and populations over the terms for providing protection and local security and/or extraction of resources. Third-party donors may step in to assist the fledging state by pledging foreign aid and other sources of support.[83]

While empirical research confirms a relationship between political settlements and DDR, less is known about the empirical relationship between political settlements and SSR.[84] No research has established causal links on the types of war settlement that affect post-conflict state capacity building. To understand how different political settlements affect SSR programming, it is important to consider the *processes* involved in state restoration.

During a transition process, a centralizing state begins to fill some of the space formerly occupied by non-state irregular factions. The centralizing state is normally required to weaken other armed groups progressively to attain (and maintain) the balance of power.[85] These statebuilding tasks include neutralizing irregular/organized non-state armed actors and deliberate policy action to reduce their authority in the political arena. States will be compelled to establish control of territory and collect weapons from potential rivals (if not acquiescing to powerful local power-brokers) to impose order over newly reacquired territories. Central states may depend on coercion in certain localities and bargaining in others (depending on the state's relationship with individual communities and the costs associated with these efforts).[86] While the processes associated with the tasks are never fully realized or complete (and therefore cannot be seen in absolute terms), the state must maintain, at a minimum, the balance of power over the means of coercion, and develop internal capacity to extend its authority and perform basic statehood functions to restore itself as the sole political authority capable of legitimately using force. There may be a situation where the costs of acquiring and/or maintaining a monopoly over violence in specific localities is too high, which obliges the central state to subcontract local security groups to perform policing duties on its behalf. There are other cases where a central state acquiesces to certain groups holding on to their organized means of coercion.

As the central state authority is being restored (usually first in the capital city and the formal institutions of the state), the balance of forces within the ruling coalition plays a role in shaping a transition period. These relations are slippery and change according to evolving power dynamics in relation to the political settlement that underpins state power.[87] The political settlement may be characterized by a weak coalition government with an unstable power-sharing arrangement dominated by leaders from the warring factions (as in Liberia).[88] Additionally, an institutionally weak government may lack the necessary material ability to extend its infrastructure and implement policies on its own behalf, and would require outside assistance to augment or propagate its domestic power (as in Sierra Leone). The state's relative power and material capabilities therefore need to be taken into account.

Thirdly, the nature of state authority at the conclusion of a war is a critical variable for DDR and SSR. The material and economic resource strength of the state is highly relevant for state restoration and likely plays a role in shaping the degree of international support.[89] A central state's relative strength will depend on its resources and general development, its capacity to control its resources and extract resources from society, and its institutional capacity to manage those resources. In contrast to governments in other regions, African governments tend to acquire capital from two major sources: development aid and profits from natural resource extraction.[90] In short, the central state's relative strength can be measured in terms of the resources at its disposal to overcome collective action problems, including those related to disarmament mentioned above. In contexts where one or more of the warring factions militarily defeats its rivals and becomes the state (as in Côte d'Ivoire in April 2011), the country's resources will shape that state's capabilities to implement the peace on its own terms.

However, a central state's capacity to overcome collective action problems also depends on existing power configurations within the ruling coalition. These power relations are often fluid arrangements based on unstable alliances that evolve dynamically in accordance with the behaviour of dominant leaders and their responses to the political environment. The crucial variable is the degree of unity within the coalition, and how this affects the state's capacity to overcome collective action. The difficulty in measuring the balance of power makes it challenging to determine how it directly affects DDR and SSR implementation.

In terms of third-party actors, the kind and amount of resources and commitment provided by external actors can potentially make a difference during transition processes. According to Doyle and Sambanis, external commitments are primarily material resources.[91] However, this emphasis on the instrumentality of resources takes the relative degree of external influence for granted and thus eliminates power relations from the discussion. The amount of resources provided by external actors is likely to affect their relative power to influence the preferences of domestic players in some post-conflict contexts. Where external influence is high in relation to state power, it may be more accurate to consider external peacebuilders as "players" rather than "referees".[92]

It is important to unpack the different actors involved, distinguish between different forms of involvement and decipher the relative influence of different donors in fragile aid-recipient societies.[93] In particular, it is vital to distinguish types of involvement and levels of commitment by different external actors throughout the process, and their potential and actual influence to shape power dynamics within the state and/or the domestic policy arena.[94]

The relative influence of donors in shaping the post-conflict statebuilding agenda will be partially determined by the resources brought to bear. Different forms of assistance include external security guarantees, international aid transfers and technical support or expatriate advisers, among others. Economic resources are crucial for DDR and SSR, as DDR and rebuilding military and police forces are extremely expensive.[95] In post-conflict African economies there is often a high degree of dependence on external material resources to implement DDR and SSR, which will likely enhance the donors' degree of influence over certain policy-making decisions.

Additionally, the nature or degree of commitment from international donors may be important for the policy-making process in statebuilding. There may be a lead state driving international policy-making in one or several major sectors. For example, Sierra Leone featured a lead-state approach involving the United Kingdom driving the statebuilding agenda.[96] In other contexts, multiple international actors have agreed on a burden-sharing approach involving donors dedicated to reform of separate sectors (as in Afghanistan). Depending on the relative power of the state *vis-à-vis* non-state rivals and international donors (based on a range of factors noted above), the central state or international donors will assume an upper hand in policy-making functions related to DDR and SSR. In the process of carrying out policy-making functions, international actors can influence internal statebuilding processes, and possibly affect power relations within the state.[97] In the context of first-order statebuilding tasks like the neutralization of irregular and state warring factions and the reconstruction and reform of state security institutions, it is important to disaggregate and analyse the various roles that external donors assume, discern their actual and potential influence over policy-making and gauge their ability to alter power relations.

While third-party actors that are perceived as neutral can play an important role in reducing uncertainty and distrust among the factions' leaders[98] under certain circumstances, these efforts depend on acquiring accurate and credible information on the specfic situation and the wider socio-political context.[99] While mediation efforts are constrained by challenges in securing credible commitments from power-brokers within the context of formal negotiations, their goal is to attain a higher degree of predictability.

Lastly, a transition process is shaped by what can be called local capacities for change. Doyle and Sambanis define local capacities for change in post-civil war contexts as the basic macro-economic development condition (GDP per capita income) and economic and social development indicators. More broadly, they consider infrastructural needs and damage caused.[100] The duration of the war, the level of hostilities and the level of destruction during the war can shape local capacities.[101] This conception of capacities is arguably vague and imprecise, because at best it can provide an indication of the developmental potential of that country after the war ends. But importantly, it does not account for the way in which states manage their resources. More precise indicators are needed for assessing local capacities for change.

Research methodology
Given the above discussion on the need for careful consideration of the chronology of events involved in state restoration, a process-tracing methodology based on two small-n comparative case studies was employed in this study.[102] This facilitates a discussion of both the substance and the process of how DDR and SSR interacted in respective contexts of state restoration and statebuilding. The next two sections elaborate on these arguments through an exploration of DDR and SSR experiences in Sierra Leone and Liberia. These two case studies draw on primary sources collected from archival research and confidential interviews with a range of African and international officials with first-hand experience in the respective DDR and SSR programmes.

DDR And SSR in Sierra Leone

This section links the previous discussion on the four dimensions critical in a post-conflict political environment to the case of Sierra Leone. The transition period starting from the July 1999 Lomé peace accord initially featured a power-sharing political settlement between the government and the Revolutionary United Front (RUF). Political power in the state was consolidated in one mainstream political party, the Sierra Leone People's Party (SLPP), and the RUF was included in a "national unity" government. However, the political settlement was under threat by irregular factions holding on to their arms and territory in the outskirts of Freetown, and other excluded armed elements in the country. A large international intervention was deployed to Sierra Leone beginning in late 1999 to support the consolidation of peace and security and strengthen the "unity" government. A more durable political settlement was eventually forged between May and September 2000 after British and Guinean military forces neutralized the remaining rebel militia forces.

The case illustrates several key aspects of the DDR–SSR relationship, particularly in relation to how evolving political settlements shape incentives for a state to engage in particular post-conflict statebuilding tasks. It features a country that attracted considerable interest among international donors to implement SSR and DDR in the state restoration process. Due to the relative weakness of the central state, DDR and SSR interventions featured prominently in peacebuilding from 2000 to 2010. External actors (notably the UK, the UN and the World Bank) designed various components of the Sierra Leonean DDR programmes from 1998 to 2004, while major aspects of the SSR programme were designed and implemented by the UK government from 1998 to 2008.

The war-to-peace transition in Sierra Leone

Over the course of Sierra Leone's decade-long civil war several irregular factions and splinter groups emerged from the army, the RUF and the pro-government civil defence forces (CDF).[103] Failed efforts to establish a political settlement throughout the 1990s resulted in a prolonged 11-year crisis.[104] One of the turning points in the conflict occurred during February–March 1998 when the ECOWAS Monitoring Group (ECOMOG) military intervention successfully mounted an offensive to dislodge the joint Armed Forces Revolutionary Council (AFRC)/RUF junta[105] from its positions in Freetown. This resulted in the restoration of the democratically elected President Tejan Kabbah. After the rebel alliance attacked Freetown in early 1999, a political accommodation was sought between the government and the RUF, leading to the Lomé peace negotiations. Under the terms of the negotiated settlement concluded in July 1999, the RUF/AFRC alliance received four full cabinet posts (two senior and two junior ministerial portfolios) and four deputy ministerial positions. RUF leader Foday Sankoh was given a position equivalent to the vice president and placed in charge of the country's natural resources, while the AFRC leader Johnny Paul Koroma became the chair of the new Commission for the Consolidation of Peace. The agreement granted "absolute and free pardon and reprieve to all combatants and collaborators"[106] guilty of atrocities and crimes committed during the war. It also provided for the DDR of all combatants and the restructuring of the military.

However, the underlying political settlement remained precarious, as different groups of warring factions held on to their arms, in particular the RUF/AFRC factions. They controlled territory in Kailahun, Kono and the northern towns of Makeni and Kabala. In October 1999 the UN established a new peacekeeping operation in Sierra Leone (UNAMSIL), incorporating the previous observer mission (UNOMIL). UNAMSIL's primary responsibility was to help implement the peace agreement and the DDR programme. The RUF capitalized on a temporary vacuum created during ECOMOG's withdrawal and UNAMSIL deployment in April 2000, abducting some UN peacekeepers. Intelligence sources suggested that the RUF was on its way to attack Freetown to take control of government. Demonstrators gathered outside the RUF leader's premises in Freetown on 6 May 2000 to protest the RUF's hostage-taking, and things soon turned violent, resulting in the deaths of over 20 protesters. These incidents gave a pretext for the government to issue an arrest warrant for Sankoh, leading eventually to his capture and the arrest of approximately 400 RUF members in Freetown (including the cabinet members in government).[107] These incidents represented the beginning of the end for the RUF.

Immediately thereafter, British troops deployed around Lungi international airport and with the help of the former AFRC leader mobilized pro-government elements in the army to save the UN mission from collapse.[108] British military forces took control of the existing remnants of the Sierra Leone Army (SLA) from the Nigerians and initiated a series of training exercises. Meanwhile, the remaining RUF commanders turned their attention to Guinea. A small group of RUF launched an incursion into Guinea, which resulted in their embarrassing defeat in September 2000 and diminished the group's fighting capacity.[109]

In May 2000 a group of former AFRC soldiers rejected their exclusion from the peace agreement, demanding a special accord with the government to re-enter the military.[110] Based in a remote jungle hideout, these ex-soldiers mounted attacks on civilians and commercial vehicles in an attempt to enhance their bargaining power with the government. The government viewed the group as illegitimate and denounced them for committing offences and criminal acts which endanger the State and peaceful citizens. During a cabinet meeting in August 2000, the government decided to withdraw the blanket amnesty provided to all combatants who "commit an offence" against the state. Although the Kabbah state was certainly "weak", it used the threat of prosecution to rein in some of the uncontrolled soldiers. The so-called West Side Boys, a splinter faction of the AFRC, came under heavy pressure, which prompted them to take 11 British soldiers and one Sierra Leonean military captain hostage in August 2000. This led to a British military intervention (Operation Barrass) that neutralized the group and resulted in the detention of all of its remaining members.[111]

The Kabbah government[112] thus gained the upper hand over all armed rivals by late 2000. Due mainly to the precarious standing of the state,[113] a large international intervention was conceptualized in Sierra Leone. International actors brought government leaders and military commanders to Abuja in November 2000 to conclude final arrangements to end the war. In the meantime, Kabbah's government sought to weaken further the RUF and other internal dissenters. The extensive UN peacekeeping presence backed by British, American and World

Bank financial and discursive resources decisively altered the balance of power in favour of the democratically elected Kabbah government.[114] The UN troops deployed in the country in March 2001 focused on enhancing state security and promoting human security.[115] Two months later, with the signing of the Abuja II accord, the disarmament process resumed for the RUF and pro-government CDF. These changing security and political conditions demonstrate the changing and revocable nature of political settlements, which in Sierra Leone's case gave the government a decisive upper hand in the peace process.

While political power was now consolidated in one mainstream political party, President Kabbah's mandate from the 1996 elections formally ended in March 2001, but had to be extended due to the underlying insecurity in the country.[116] After the signing of the Abuja II accord on 15 May 2001, the international community focused its attention on disarmament in preparation for holding elections scheduled for late 2001.[117] Within this context, DDR was rolled out nationally in May 2001, largely on terms defined by the UN and donors, with government input.

DDR: Institutions and incentives

To understand how "DDR" interacted within this political space and how local political processes influenced its form and substance, it is important to consider the incentives and constraints faced by the Kabbah state, on the one hand, and the remaining commanders of the irregular factions on the other. The third phase of the DDR programme ran from mid-May 2001 to early January 2002.[118] The robust UNAMSIL peacekeeping force was deployed throughout Sierra Leone in tandem with the DDR programme. In early 2001 attention focused on disarming the remaining RUF forces. At the time, the RUF and CDF were based in different districts across the country. To facilitate a process for disarmament, a special commander incentive programme was conceptualized that targeted the remaining RUF and CDF leaders.[119] The RUF leaders had an incentive to cooperate: they had been militarily defeated, and the special reintegration package promised to the leaders was conditional on good behaviour.[120]

UN mediators established a disarmament negotiation process on two levels: political and technical/field. At the political level, the National Commission for Disarmament, Demobilization and Reintegration (NCDDR) was a coordinating institution in charge of DDR on behalf of the fledging government. A team of international advisers from the World Bank and UN Development Programme

(UNDP) was embedded in the NCDDR to ensure effective management of the process from May 2001 to 2004.[121] The Tripartite (composed of high-level representatives of the government, political leaders and UNAMSIL) and technical coordinating committees (TCCs) facilitated cooperation and coordination between the different actors involved in the design and implementation of the DDR programme. Their work was geared towards directly and indirectly enhancing the Kabbah state's policy formulation and implementation capacity while reducing the chances that loosely coordinated remnants of the RUF could disrupt the peace. Kabbah took an active interest and direct role in the DDR programme during its initial phases as *de facto* head of the NCDDR. He established a presidential taskforce following the Lomé peace accord to discuss its implementation, including the DDR programme. President Kabbah presided over taskforce meetings held on 10 and 14 May 2001, to prepare his government and solicit international support through foreign aid. Although international donors maintained control of the Multi-Donor Trust Fund, which financed the DDR programme,[122] Kabbah's government insisted on having access to small tranches that could be used at its discretion to overcome delays in donor funding. External actors insisted that the government take ownership of DDR-related policies and strategies, to the greatest extent possible.[123]

Through the NCDDR, Sierra Leonean government authorities and World Bank and UNDP staff played active behind-the-scenes roles in policy-making for the DDR programmes, some of which had relevance for the concurrent British-funded SSR programme (SILSEP). The Kabbah state had an interest in using some elements of DDR to consolidate its power, so it established thoughtful position statements on the MRP for former SLA soldiers, locations of demobilization centres, acceptance criteria for combatants entering DDR (group versus individual, weapons handover, etc.) and reintegration options, and endorsed a revised UN DDR joint operation plan with a handful of its own reservations.[124] As the security gains for the government accumulated, the government and the World Bank recruited a Sierra Leonean administrator to take over as head of the NCDDR Secretariat. The president was able to withdraw from his role as the head of the NCDDR to focus on wider state priorities.

The NCDDR's work was also driven by the Tripartite, which discussed emergent challenges related to ceasefire violations, the release of prisoners of war and donor involvement, among others. It included cabinet members, members of the NCDDR, RUF and CDF political leaders, and key UNAMSIL military and civilian officials. Chaired by the UN special representative to the Secretary-General

(SRSG) and advised by representatives of key international donors (such as the UK high commissioner and the US ambassador), the Tripartite was dominated by the most powerful outside donors. The executive secretary of the NCDDR (a Sierra Leonean) served as the secretary of the Tripartite, and it was useful for signalling intentions between the RUF and government[125] and negotiating formal and informal constraints and incentives that became the framework for two-tier political negotiations to disarm the RUF.[126] From May 2001 to January 2002 eight Tripartite meetings were held. Aside from a few minor setbacks, the Tripartite was efficient in overcoming the key policy and political challenges that hindered effective implementation of DDR. It is important to underline that implementation of disarmament was relatively efficient in large part because a fairly coherent central government was in place, along with a political pact with the remaining RUF leaders and strong international commitment.

To ensure top-down and bottom-up coherence for disarmament, several mechanisms were established to facilitate political and field-level negotiations. One mechanism was the integration of "liaison officers" from both the RUF and the CDF in the NCDDR Executive Secretariat.[127] Once the process gathered momentum in mid-2001, six junior commanders from each of the three warring factions were integrated as liaison officers to assist in the implementation of DDR in the NCDDR's regional offices after May–June 2001.[128] The liaison officers reported back to their factions' command structure during the DDR process, and in some cases worked together with UNAMSIL and local leaders to form local peace committees. Their role was critical for verifying and validating the identity of demobilized combatants during the reintegration phase.[129]

At the technical/field level the TCCs were established to discuss policy affecting local implementation of DDR. The UNAMSIL force commander, deputy force commander, chief military observer, the chief of staff and the senior DDR staff in UNAMSIL led the TCCs' work. The TCCs had local-level field-based problem-solving committees chaired by UNAMSIL military observers (MILOBS) that met on a weekly basis (usually every Friday) to review concerns in the political and security environment that directly affected the DDR operations.[130] The TCCs aimed to implement the policies agreed by the Tripartite on issues relating to scheduling and logistics.[131] The principal links between UNAMSIL and the local RUF and CDF commanders were the MILOBS and officials from the UN DDR cell. These actors played important problem-solving roles in an evolving context to address logistical constraints affecting the implementation of disarmament and demobilization, including investigating ceasefire violations and sensitization visits to ensure disarmament continued.[132] Members of the TCCs negotiated the final disarmament schedule and made recommendations to the Tripartite on any changes to the timeline. An important aspect of this work involved negotiating and consulting with the local commanders to finalize details related to the logistics for disarmament at the district level. This was essential, since irregular forces' commanders on the ground acted as gatekeepers to combatants before their release for disarmament and demobilization. Policy issues that emerged in the field were sometimes elevated to higher forums such as the Tripartite, depending on the sensitivity of the issue.[133] In late 2001 UNAMSIL announced that about 45,000 combatants had been disarmed, and the government declared the war officially over in early January 2002.[134]

In the context of the DDR programme, Kabbah's government was restored as the only legitimate authority capable of using force. The government capitalized on the success achieved by the UN DDR programme by designing its own community arms collection and destruction (CACD) programme in October 2001. Again, the Kabbah state had an interest in – and, with the help of the UN, the capacity to pursue – a programme to disarm the civilian population.[135] Designed by members of the Sierra Leonean Ministry of Internal Affairs with input from the police, the programme aimed not only to collect all remaining arms from civilians but to pursue SSR-related issues to enhance the system for regulating and licensing all arms and ammunition in the country.

The CACD was implemented at the district and chiefdom levels in the final months of the UN DDR programme.[136] From December 2001 to April 2002 recently retrained members of the Sierra Leone Police (SLP) implemented the CACD programme, and specifically focused on collecting weapons in the possession of the CDF that were beyond the UN's criteria for disarmament, notably single-barrel hunting rifles and pistols.[137] Civilians were "required to voluntarily submit all arms, ammunition and explosives in their possession within a specified period during which an amnesty will be granted".[138] The CACD depended on the support of paramount chiefs to "actively encourage the population within their chiefdoms" to submit their arms and locate hidden arms caches through community networks.[139] After the specified amnesty period (usually eight weeks), the SLP conducted limited cordon and search operations "in close consultation and collaboration with UNAMSIL".[140] The SLP and Ministry of Internal Affairs invoked the country's firearms legislation, two ordinances previously established before the war.[141] Threats of prosecution were used as a powerful motivator to encourage weapon handovers. According to the government, any person found in possession of arms, ammunition and explosives after the specified period could be "subject to criminal proceedings and subsequent prosecution".[142]

In the end, the community disarmament programme collected 9,237 arms and a total of 34,035 pieces of ammunition and explosives.[143] As a key component, any functioning small arms were stored in police-monitored depots around the country with the help of UNAMSIL, which also played an important role in destroying some of the unusable weapons and ammunition that were collected.[144]

Key outside actors (Britain, the United States and the UN) capitalized on this enhanced security environment to support presidential and parliamentary elections in May 2002.[145] By the end of March 2002 there were 17,455 UN peacekeepers deployed throughout Sierra Leone, which allowed elections to be conducted.[146] Tejan Kabbah's re-election in May 2002 left little doubt over who was in power.[147]

SSR, democratic governance and state consolidation

After ascertaining the process by which a central state authority was restored during the transition, and DDR's role in this process, this subsection addresses the relationship between international SSR and efforts to consolidate the state and enhance its "democratic governance". As previously mentioned, the fact that political power was consolidated in one political party made it easier for the British to support the Kabbah government to overcome critical collective action problems in the security realm. Immediately following the May 2002 elections, the government of Sierra Leone signed a memorandum of understanding (MOU) with the UK government which committed the UK to a 10-year peacebuilding partnership. First, a political settlement between Kabbah and the various elements in the Sierra Leone military had to be forged by extensive UK involvement.[148] Second, while seeking to prop up the Sierra Leonean state after the 2002 elections through direct budget support and international development and security assistance, UK statebuilders insisted that the Kabbah state improve the transparency and accountability of the government in the delivery of security and social provisions. The UK government invested significantly in SSR, specifically in the SLP and military as core pillars of Sierra Leone's state reconstruction process and in the government's poverty reduction strategy. A core group of 150 trainers from the British-led International Military Advisory Training Team (IMATT) focused on improving the state's capacity to control its legitimate use of force through retraining and restructuring of the SLA. Meanwhile, IMATT worked with the UN to address the issue of civil and military reintegration on the one hand, and SLP retraining and restructuring on the other.[149]

Forging a political settlement with the army

The relative weakness of the Sierra Leonean state, particularly Kabbah's inability to establish a unified command within the police and army to "hold together" the political settlement, was one of the main reasons for the expansive UK-led SSR intervention in Sierra Leone.[150] Several channels were created to facilitate the UK's direct involvement in the country's security sector. First, British advisers were deployed to Sierra Leone and embedded in key government bodies. For instance, a small team of UK Ministry of Defence (MOD) advisers was engaged in policy-making functions in a new Sierra Leonean MOD from 1999 to 2002, then expanded in scope and personnel from 2002 to 2007. UK military officers from IMATT also effectively took control of key functions within the newly established MOD and the SLA, reconstituted in 2002 as the Republic of Sierra Leone Armed Forces (RSLAF). Additionally, UK military officers were embedded in commanding positions in the RSLAF, including at the operational level through the Joint Force Command, the Joint Support Command, brigade and battalion commanders, and the Armed Forces Training Centre and Officers Academy.[151] Britain provided all the funds for restructuring the RSLAF (through the Africa Conflict Prevention Pool) and 80–90 per cent of the IMATT personnel.

One of the "first-order" tasks involved consolidating control of the existing army personnel and creating some semblance of a unified command. While some 9,500–11,500 soldiers and officers remained on the army pay list in June 2000, the "national" army was divided between three main factions: a pro-Kabbah coalition of SLA figures, ex-SLA personnel and Kamajor fighters (a security force composed of traditional hunters from the Mende ethnic group). Up to this time, control of the SLA had fallen on the shoulders of a Nigerian brigadier as chief of defence staff. The British military took over this responsibility from the Nigerians in May 2000. At the time it would have been arguably impossible for Kabbah to gain control of all of these factions, let alone develop a credible mechanism to coordinate their war-fighting efforts. British military commanders reduced the costs that would have been incurred had Kabbah been required to organize the military on his own. A core group of about 3,700 existing soldiers and officers were actively involved in assisting ECOMOG's war-fighting efforts against the RUF in 1999. These soldiers and officers were organized into three battalions by the Nigerians to assist the regional ECOMOG peacekeeping force to fight the AFRC/RUF alliance during the attacks on Freetown in early January 1999.[152] The existing army received British short-term training between 1999 and August 2000.[153] One of the first mechanisms for the UK SILSEP I team to gain control of the SLA was to resume pay for the soldiers, around December 1999.[154] Under British supervision, a nominal roll call was conducted in early January 2000 which registered approximately 3,720 personnel.[155] On 12 August 2000 a second nominal call was conducted by the British (deadline extended to 28 August), which required all military personnel to reregister for the army.[156] The UK-led military mission focused on retraining Sierra Leone military personnel, implementing an MRP and introducing new incentive systems within the MOD and RSLAF.

SSR and democratic governance

The MOU agreement called on the UK to provide material assistance in direct budget support and lead the Sierra Leone police and military reform processes, as well as to provide material support for the creation of new central state institutions such as the Office of National Security, Central Intelligence and Security Unit and Anti-Corruption Commission. The UK's overarching focus was to shore up the capacity of the government of Sierra Leone and expand its presence in the countryside (through redeployment of chiefs, civil administrators and police). The tasks and timing of external support were largely structured around achieving an exit strategy for the UN peacekeeping force according to certain key benchmarks.

The UK's initial bilateral SSR intervention in Sierra Leone focused on defence and security institutions, including standard "train-and-equip" and force-modernization elements. The approach later evolved into a broader focus on improving the governance of the security sector, including modernizing the legal framework in which security actors operate and strengthening oversight of these institutions, particularly the MOD and parliament. Extensive efforts were made to improve Sierra Leone's national security architecture, including establishing new national security institutions, introducing new legislation and improving security management through ministerial reform.[157] These efforts aimed to lay some foundation for democratic governance in the security sector.

IMATT envisioned a three- to five-year programme involving a complete overhaul of the MOD and the military apparatus as part of a process to establish appropriate civilian oversight of the armed forces.[158] At least nine IMATT officers remained in the new post-war MOD after its formal opening in January 2002.[159] During this period (2003–2004), IMATT focused on "stabilization" of the RSLAF command through various measures, including leadership and collective training exercises.[160] Kabbah had an interest in supporting a strong UNAMSIL and IMATT presence in the country to improve security, restart economic activity and consolidate state control of the armed forces.

Earlier, in Commonwealth and British-led SLP restructuring in 1998–1999, efforts were made to lay the groundwork for a substantive revision of the SLP's policing practices, training and recruitment. British police officials were deeply involved in commanding positions in the SLP. The UK's Department for International Development and Foreign and Commonwealth Office funded the programme, with a focus on redefining the SLP's role, composition and training, the mechanisms for oversight and conditions of service. Kabbah appointed a British national as the highest-ranking police officer (inspector-general), who was firmly in control of key aspects of Sierra Leone's police reform from October 1999 until 2003.[161] Significant restructuring of the SLP took place from 2000 to 2002, including retraining of existing personnel and recruitment of new officers.

Thus a unique feature of both military and police reform programmes was the ability to induce change through direct involvement of external actors in the security apparatus and the emphasis on reform and oversight.

DDR–SSR links

The civilian reintegration programme, which targeted ex-combatants for civilian livelihoods, was accelerated by the NCDDR after the 2002 election, lasting for a maximum of two years up to 2004. The civilian and military reintegration components were ongoing simultaneously from 2001 to 2004, when SSR was implemented. Thus of interest for this study are possible realized (or missed) synergies or overlaps in their programming.[162] From a temporal point of view, there was a short period when the respective DDR and SSR processes overlapped. The DDR intervention lasted less than three years, from May 2001 until 2004, while the SSR process lasted more than a decade through different phases from about 1999 (while police reform was under way) until around 2012–2013. The core overlapping period occurred before and following May 2001 (after the signing of the second Abuja accord) until mid-May 2002. This section focuses on this period to identify a chronology of events and discern whether links were established in the DDR and SSR programmes.

DDR–SSR links at the policy level

As mentioned, the 2009 IDDRS module on DDR and SSR identifies the formation of national security policies, integration and information sharing as potential opportunities where links can be established between DDR and SSR. While it is impossible to cover all the national security policy planning that occurred after the war, a few core issues are worth mentioning. During this period, the government was considering proposals to establish a territorial defence force out of some of the CDF, particularly the southeastern-based Kamajors, who were pro-government and closely aligned with Kabbah's SLPP. The head of the CDF was Kabbah's deputy minister of defence, the retired army captain Hinga Norman, who was actively involved in early military reform in 1999 and the disarmament of the CDF in 2001.[163] However, President Kabbah was dissuaded from creating a territorial force to police the borders modelled after the British territorial force because of the long-term security implications of maintaining both an irregular paramilitary-style army and the regular army. This idea was eventually discarded following the 2002 elections, and Kabbah shifted Norman to the Ministry of Interior and retained the position of minister of defence to ensure the British military would have full control of RSLAF reforms. Instead, many of the CDF fighters went through DDR or simply self-integrated into their chiefdoms.

Another relevant policy decision was whether to reintegrate old soldiers who had been recruited before and during the war into the army. Around November 1999 the government (through the NCDDR) developed a policy stating that all ex-combatants must be disarmed and demobilized by a third-party peacekeeper force, after which they could opt for either the civilian reintegration programme or enter a recruitment programme for the national army. Those unable or unwilling to enter the military would be automatically considered for the civilian reintegration programme.[164]

On 16 December 1999 President Kabbah chaired a national security meeting at his presidential lodge to discuss the status of the former SLA soldiers and options for either civilian or military reintegration. The government decided to reinstate all ex-SLA soldiers back into the army except those clearly known to be unsuitable.[165] The government was uncertain about how many and which officers and soldiers would be reinstated in the army. In addition, it developed a policy stating that promotions awarded after the expulsion of the junta from Freetown in 1998 would not be recognized. Since the Kabbah-led government was particularly sensitive to the potential role that AFRC elements could play in destabilizing the transition period, it decided to open promotions made by the AFRC junta to a negotiation process. In the same vein, it agreed to pay salary arrears to all soldiers who were "eligible ... except for the period May 27th, 1997 to the time of reinstatement".[166]

The British advisers and the Sierra Leonean government developed an NCDDR policy framework and process for screening ex-combatants for the army. First, combatants who wished to be considered for integration in the army were required to express an interest at the end of demobilization. Their names were submitted by UN military personnel to the MOD for consideration in the army. Irregular combatants and military personnel were screened by UK and Sierra Leone defence officials; those who did not meet the established criteria were permitted to return to the civilian DDR process and were entitled to receive a demobilization and reintegration assistance package as well as a pension/gratuity from the government in accordance with the terms and conditions of their service.

The British government capitalized on the fact that a team from the UK MOD was already deployed to Freetown as embedded staff in Sierra Leone's MOD. The team of three military personnel and civilians led by Colonel Mike Dent drafted policies for the new force structure and strength, and developed strategies for basing requirements.[167] A few weeks after the Lomé accord was signed (7 July 1999), the UK military team began drawing up plans to establish an 8,600-strong army, build a new Defence Ministry headquarters (moving the MOD office to a hotel lot adjacent to the State House) and create a new joint support command and armed forces personnel centre at defence headquarters. From late 1999 and early January 2000, Britain deployed an SSR team (SILSEP) to Freetown to ramp up efforts to envision the military reconstruction programme.[168]

DDR–SSR links in military and police integration programmes
There is no publicly available evidence indicating any practical links between the DDR programme and the SLP recruitment process. The British Inspector-General Keith Biddle insisted on avoiding deals with the ex-RUF to integrate some of them directly into the police. Although the UN Civilian Police (CivPol) officers supported the idea of permitting former combatants to join the police force as a way to employ youth who had fought during the war, Biddle convinced President Kabbah to avoid an integration programme for the SLP, arguing that this would undermine the ethos of the new police force.[169] In mid-2001, when the DDR programme was rolling out, Biddle initiated a nationwide recruitment drive for the SLP. Biddle worked with the assistant inspector-generals to reconfigure the recruitment procedures in an effort to professionalize the force and reduce

the likelihood of politicians manipulating recruitment practices based on ethnic or political calculations.[170]

British military officers involved in RSLAF reform established links with UN and NCDRR authorities for the purpose of coordination with the DDR programme during recruitment of ex-combatants into the new RSLAF from mid-May 2001 to mid-May 2002. The integration of the warring factions into the army was first discussed during the peace talks at Lomé in July 1999.[171] Article 16 of the Lomé agreement states that all combatants and paramilitary groups, including the RUF, CDF and SLA, should be disarmed and demobilized from their respective existing military structures.[172] Article 17 states that all combatants wishing to be integrated in restructured national armed forces may do so provided they meet the "established criteria".[173] The government of Sierra Leone's 1999 policy recognized a link between the DDR programme and the restructuring of the armed forces, considering that "each is separate and follows a distinct process".[174] The Kabbah government was initially open to the idea of establishing a quota system for permitting integration of combatants in the army. However, since the government outsourced RSLAF reform to the British, it was left to the senior British military officers to decide. Their rationale was to ensure a credible and neutral process of selection in the army based on "established criteria" that could be "applied uniformly in an open and transparent manner towards combatants from all fighting forces".[175] Senior British military officers wanted to avoid politicization of the army, as much as possible. The government approved this decision, and suspended all recruitment processes "in order to provide each interested combatant the opportunity for consideration into the restructured armed forces".[176]

The British-designed MRP, implemented by IMATT in May 2001, featured strongly in the early SSR efforts.[177] The MRP was intended to "lay the foundation for future recruit training in the RSLAF as a whole".[178] Links were established at the operational level between IMATT authorities in charge of implementing the MRP and UN authorities implementing the DDR programmes. As part of IMATT's Operation Silkman, IMATT commanders maintained a communication link with the NCDDR for the purpose of information sharing, particularly when clarification was needed on the eligibility of certain discharged soldiers for DDR. For instance, combatants entering the DDR process were required to indicate immediately to UN MILOBS their interest in joining the army. IMATT personnel screened the ex-combatants. If an individual passed the initial selection tests, he/she was selected as a "potential" rank. Further testing and training were done at the platoon level. Ex-combatants were then transferred to MRP holding centres where they would undergo screening, including tests of physical fitness, basic reading and writing, and knowledge comprehension.[179] The experience in Sierra Leone demonstrates the difficulty of recruiting highly qualified individuals into a post-war army: the vast majority could not pass the basic literacy tests. However, the British officers involved in this process were extremely lenient on these restrictions. A large percentage of ex-AFRC (from those who volunteered to re-enlist in August 2000) were integrated, along with about 3,000 ex-combatants from the RUF and CDF.[180] The majority of MRP entrants were integrated into the army as privates, lance-corporals or corporals.[181] If at any stage an ex-combatant failed a test and was discharged, he/she was eligible to receive the DDR benefits. The IMATT liaisons remained in regular contact with the NCDDR and UNAMSIL's DDR cell to ensure that those discharged would qualify for reintegration benefits.

At the officer corps level, "all potential officers sat a series of examinations designed to select those candidates best suited for further training on the RLSAF Commissioning Course".[182] Additionally, all candidates sat before an interview board made up of IMATT and RSLAF officers. About 40 ex-combatants were made officers (mostly former Kamajors) and about 200 were integrated as non-commissioned officers.[183] If a "potential officer" did not pass the selection process, he/she was given the option of either staying in the RSLAF as a soldier or being discharged from the military. In the event of a discharge, IMATT officials sent an official request to the NCDDR to indicate that the individual had been discharged and was eligible for DDR programme benefits. Officials from IMATT and the NCDDR shared a common interest in preventing duplicate payments in both military and civilian reintegration programmes.

DDR–SSR links during implementation
What mechanisms linked SSR and DDR? The Sierra Leone government (through the NCDDR Executive Secretariat and MOD) worked together with civilian and military staff in UNAMSIL's DDR cell to develop a policy for ex-soldiers officially discharged from the army to benefit from the civilian DDR programme. In December 2000 NCDDR executive secretary Francis Kai-Kai requested Sierra Leone's then acting chief of defence staff, Brigadier Tom Carew, to submit a list of Sierra Leonean ex-soldiers who qualified for DDR assistance.[184] The UN insisted on good record-keeping practices and open communication between the NCDDR, UNAMSIL's DDR cell and field staff to ensure information sharing. On 27 September 1999 the NCDDR had approved a policy that all ex-SLA discharged from the army would receive support "in line with the support offered to all members of the various fighting forces".[185]

The British troops in command of IMATT also established a liaison programme with UNAMSIL, beginning in August 2000. IMATT established a DDR civil–military cooperation unit, led by a junior military officer, to liaise with the appropriate UN authorities involved in the DDR programme. As part of this programme, the British military embedded Major Michael A. Evanson-Goddard in the UNAMSIL headquarters DDR cell to help conceptualize and implement the DDR programme during its third phase (from 2001). The British officer Colonel Paul Farrar, who served as director of army training in the RSLAF, liaised with both UN civilians working on the DDR programme and civilian and military staff in UNAMSIL, on behalf of IMATT.[186]

The implementation of a screening process during the MRP does not necessarily result in effective capacity building in the army. The screening was constrained by a limited amount of information on recruits, since many of the army's personnel records were destroyed during the war. Civil society leaders claimed that the screening process developed by the British was poor, resulting in the integration of soldiers with a record of gross human rights violations, which raised concerns about the RSLAF's legitimacy in the transitional period.[187] It is fair to say that the standards for selection (in terms of assessing a recruit's psychological health and literacy level) declined significantly during the MRP.[188] However, this was considered as a fair trade-off in an effort to promote short-term reconciliation.[189] The size of the RSLAF grew to about 14,400 troops following the integration of ex-AFRC soldiers and three subsequent rounds of the MRP. The mechanisms linking the NCDDR with IMATT were crucial in the years immediately following the MRP. Recruits demobilized within the initial one-year contract were entitled to receive civilian reintegration benefits, but after that initial year such benefits were no longer available.

Main findings on the DDR–SSR relationship

The RUF's military defeat in late 2000 and the neutralization of the West Side Boys soldiers gave the Kabbah state a decisive victory at the end of the war. Due mainly to a precarious financial state of affairs, a large international intervention was conceptualized in Sierra Leone, which drastically altered the incentives system. Extensive British military engagement effectively assisted the government of Sierra Leone to capitalize on the evolving security and political conditions to assume an upper hand in the peace process in late 2000, and effectively shored up the political settlement underlying the central state. When the DDR programme was rolled out nationally in May 2001, the government (with strong international backing) had acquired the balance of power *vis-à-vis* other irregular armed groups. The Kabbah state appropriated certain elements of the UN-led DDR programme to enhance its domestic position in advance of the post-war elections held in May 2002. Despite the state's precarious financial standing, Sierra Leonean authorities engaged extensively in national policy-making in DDR and SSR-related issues during the transition process. The relevant question is why did the government embrace some elements of the international DDR and SSR programmes over others? The findings from this study suggest that the Kabbah state selectively adopted the elements that would either be useful to consolidate its *infrastructural power*[190] and establish control over territory and the population, or could enhance the state's legitimacy in the eyes of relevant international donors.

The SSR intervention occurred over a much longer time horizon – just over 10 years – well beyond the three-year DDR programme.[191] During the time overlap, several mechanisms were created to link some components of the DDR programme with the SSR programme, such as the NCDDR, Tripartite, TCCs and the CACD. Combined, these mechanisms facilitated a process of collecting arms from the irregular factions, which aided a power shift from the irregular factions to central government from mid-2000 until mid-2002. By neutralizing the remaining armed elements of the irregular factions (RUF, West Side Boys) and integrating thousands of ex-SLA and former AFRC fighters into the army, the UK supported the Kabbah state to restore itself as the sole political entity capable of legitimately using force. The integration of these factions was key to sustaining the existing political settlement. Through the post-war SSR process – which was largely directed by hands-on UK involvement and funding – the central state had an interest in supporting this programme to maintain its power and capitalize on this power shift while improving the state's security capacity in key areas of police and military reform through retraining and restructuring of the security forces. The Kabbah state saw this as an opportunity to consolidate its control of the armed forces and enhance the legitimacy of the central state.

Within this context, several mechanisms were created at the field level to facilitate cooperation between the various actors, notably IMATT, UNAMSIL and the NCDDR during the DDR and SSR interventions. These included a liaison programme between IMATT and the UNAMSIL DDR cell to ensure effective information sharing between the military and civilian reintegration programmes for both demobilized combatants seeking to enter the army and those returning to civilian life. The conditions under which these mechanisms were effectively operationalized included a sufficiently secure political and military environment (in which organized irregular factions were neutralized, backed by a strong UN peacekeeping force), and a central state authority shored up by external support that had an interest in embracing certain elements of DDR–SSR for its own Tillyean statebuilding purposes.

In short, DDR–SSR synergies depend not only on temporal overlaps but also local conditions and politics. We need to understand the contextually contingent impact that politics has on policy-making, including the nature of central state authority and its interests in embracing or undermining different DDR–SSR elements. Thus it is important to consider the relationship from both supply *and* demand perspectives, and discern whether or to what extent the state benefits from DDR–SSR interventions in pursuit of its statebuilding and political objectives.

DDR and SSR in Liberia

After more than 14 years of crisis in Liberia,[192] a military ceasefire was signed on 17 June 2003 between Liberia's minister of defence and Liberians United for Reconciliation and Democracy (LURD) military leaders.[193] This effectively created the context for subsequent political negotiations in August held in Accra, Ghana, involving the three warring factions and members of Liberia's political elite. In contrast to Sierra Leone there was no winner from the war, and the international community implemented a power-sharing agreement between the three warring factions. Liberia's early transition (2003–2005) became defined by this unstable power-sharing agreement, resulting in a highly dysfunctional two-year transitional government comprising leaders and members of the factions. Members of this government used their power to further their own agendas and jockeyed for political position in the central state among themselves and with the established political elite. Additionally, the post-conflict reconstruction process was shaped by an extensive international intervention involving a UN-led police restructuring and DDR programme and US-led military reform. The dysfunctionality of the central government opened opportunities for greater external oversight of key government institutions.

DDR and SSR featured prominently in Liberia's peacebuilding transition. External actors, notably the UN and the International Contact Group on Liberia (ICGL),[194] established the framework for the Liberian DDR programme, while major aspects of the SSR programme were designed and implemented by UN, US and Nigerian/ECOWAS authorities. DDR and SSR policy design and implementation were "muddled through" and compartmentalized by several external and internal actors. As part of the wider peacebuilding strategy, external actors sought to dismantle and neutralize the former Taylor regime's security apparatus by reforming Liberia's security sector and security-oriented institutions.[195]

This section argues that the absence of a coherent political settlement underlying the Liberian transitional government limited opportunities for joined-up policy-making on DDR and SSR issues. In regards to DDR, the prominent leaders of the three factions concentrated their efforts on accessing the "spoils" of state and were less concerned with the coordination of disarmament. In terms of SSR, the national transitional government (NTGL) viewed the development of national security strategy as outside the scope of its mandate, which was to implement the Comprehensive Peace Accord (CPA) and not to ensure "good governance". As a result, there were fewer incentives for the members of the NTGL to implement collective action projects on behalf of the central state. This led to a dearth of national strategies, at least in relation to security policies, for the duration of the time that DDR and SSR were implemented.

The war-to-peace transition in Liberia

After the military ceasefire ended the final battle for Monrovia in July 2003, a 32-member US military assessment team arrived in Monrovia on 6 July 2003 to support troops supplied by the West Africa regional body ECOWAS and try to prevent further attacks on the capital. ECOWAS held an extraordinary summit in Accra on 31 July 2003 to deal with the Liberian crisis, and passed a resolution to deploy a 3,600-strong peacekeeping force to Liberia on 4 August. The consequences of Liberia's protracted civil war for development were profound. Beyond the number of casualties, the war left a harsh legacy in the country. Forced migration, refugee flows, capital flight and the destruction of social, health and educational infrastructure were only some of the negative consequences of internal crisis. Liberia's post-war economic and social conditions were arguably worse than those in Sierra Leone.[196]

To appreciate the DDR and SSR process fully, it is important to place the post-war intervention in its proper political context. The prize for the three main irregular factions was political and military supremacy in Liberia's post-war institutions, including the executive branch of government, the ministries and parastatals and the legislative bodies, during the transition period. Intensive political jockeying occurred in the last days of the war between Taylor's former National Pariotic Front of Liberia (NPFL) forces, who were in control of the executive mansion and certain areas in Monrovia (and recognized as the government),[197] LURD, an anti-Taylor rebel force controlling some areas on the western outskirts of Monrovia,[198] and the Movement for Democracy in Liberia (MODEL),[199] also an anti-Taylor movement based in the southeast.[200]

Political negotiations in mid-June 2003 and early August 2003 concluded with the signing of the CPA on 18 August 2003.[201] A defining characteristic of Liberia's transition process was the fact that these factions became the state. Liberia's power-sharing framework divided political power equally among the three factions. The CPA called for the establishment of a two-year transitional government as an interim measure until presidential elections could be held in October 2005.

The NTGL consisted of an executive and cabinet, the legislative assembly, a judiciary and government commissions.[202] To prevent any one faction from heading the government, two political party leaders, Gyude Bryant (a former chair of the Liberian Action Party in 1992) and Wesley Johnson (member of the United People's Party), were selected as the interim chair and vice-chair.[203] The balance of forces within the NTGL involved a complex configuration with key government ministries divided up among the leaders of the three factions, while eight ministerial positions were allocated to members of the country's political parties and seven to "civil society".[204] Each of the three factions was given control of one of the strategic ministerial positions, while the remaining ministerial posts were given to representatives from political parties and civil society groups.[205]

While the mediator's intention was to give the political parties and civil society the balance of power in the transitional state, power continued to be concentrated among the senior leaders of the three former factions. The transitional state was institutionally weak and lacked competencies in performing basic policy-making tasks. Since the power-sharing arrangement underlying the NTGL lasted for only two years, there were very few, if any, incentives for ministers to think long term. There were few functioning financial management policies introduced in the state or self-enforcing constraints on self-maximizing and predatory behaviour by the NTGL officials. Although this varied across the different ministries and parastatals, some leaders of the factions continued their rent-seeking practices through control of the state apparatus.[206] The power-sharing arrangement and the broader institutional context proved too unstable to permit the effective functioning of government business. The first year of the transition process (January 2004–January 2005) proved highly dysfunctional, and by the end of the year the NTGL was imploding from within.[207]

Since there was no national army or police force to provide equitable security in November–December 2003, a 3,700-strong ECOMOG military force stationed in Monrovia was in charge of manning checkpoints and strategic posts. This force was to be reinforced by the peacekeeping mission for Liberia (UNMIL) approved by the UN Security Council in September 2003, comprising approximately 15,000 UN peacekeeping personnel (both military and police). After the final battle that ended the war, the majority of the remaining fighters were based in Monrovia. While there was no central authority to impose order or implement disarmament, there was an existing structure of power that resembled some sense of order in Monrovia.[208] The first puzzle was to determine how to restore the state as the sole political authority capable of legitimately using force.

UNMIL, led by Special Representative Jacques Klein, problematically assumed that local capacities in Liberia were non-existent.[209] Senior officials from the UN Department of Peacekeeping Operations (DPKO) and UNMIL designed the DDR programme in November 2003 without consulting any of the leaders of the warring factions or the Liberian officials from the National Commission for Disarmament, Demobilization, Rehabilitation and Reintegration (NCDDRR). With only 5,000 troops stationed in Monrovia by 1 December, Klein pushed a timeline to disarm the estimated 40,000 combatants from the three factions. It was simply assumed that the Accra accord was a sufficient condition to implement disarmament on the leaders' behalf. Despite being warned by local commanders that this would fail, the UN insisted on moving ahead with its imposed schedule.[210] On 1 December a symbolic disarmament kicked off in Monrovia in advance of the scheduled start on 7 December. Despite being warned again by the commanders and senior leaders of the factions on 5 December, the UN pushed the original timeline. On 7 December approximately 14,000 combatants (mostly male youth from Taylor's militia forces) brought their arms to the designated cantonment site at Camp Sheffelin.[211] Combatants were told they would receive US$300 cash immediately upon handing over their weapons to a UN soldier. The camp lacked basic provisions such as water, shelter and food, and suddenly became chaotic when some combatants got restive and frustrated after learning they would only receive half the cash promised to them.[212] One combatant fired into the air, resulting in an eruption of armed violence.[213] Thousands of battled-hardened combatants exited the camp in mass numbers, which led to riots in the streets and at least nine deaths.

Klein consulted with senior members of Taylor's government, notably Vice President Moses Blah and Defence Minister Daniel Chea, to bring order to the situation. Chea instructed his key senior commanders (Coco Denis and Roland Duo) to organize an informal force of about 30–40 men to stop the violence and forcefully disarm the thousands of combatants roaming the streets, looting homes, stealing property and harassing people in Monrovia. The pro-Taylor militia forces restored basic order in Monrovia by 27 December 2003,[214] thus creating some time and space for international actors on the ground to establish the NTGL as the sole authority capable of legitimately using force. However, the NTGL still remained divided along factional lines and lacked a "national" orientation, as shown in the next subsection. The central state authority (which itself was unstable) lacked an incentive to start a coherent and unified national policy-making process. To a limited extent the MOD did engage in some policy and planning initiatives, but these were eventually discarded in favour of a US plan.

During this reconstruction process, the US government took the lead within UN Security Council matters related to Liberia and in the International Contact Group. In contrast to the British approach in Sierra Leone, the US government preferred to keep at "arm's length" on the ground to share the burden and costs of peacebuilding, so it worked through UNMIL and assumed leadership positions in the peacekeeping mission.[215] The UN's role was to support the NTGL to implement the CPA, and lead in the preparation and organization of elections in October 2005. The ICGL decided to step in and assume *de facto* control of Liberia's economic institutions in late 2005.[216] The UN brought enormous material and discursive resources to the extremely poor setting of Liberia. Indeed, in both Sierra Leone and Liberia the best jobs and biggest contracts came from the UN, and the injection of capital for development and DDR-related projects provided an immediate incentive to exploit for a range of different local actors.[217]

When the NTGL's internal dysfunctionality became clear to the donors, the World Bank and the US government introduced more extensive measures to contain corruption and alter incentives within the Liberian state to prevent rent-seeking. International technocrats and judges were recruited in core national institutions to handle policy-making and set up administrative procedures on behalf of the "state". The most important state economic institutions were targeted for external oversight in an arrangement called the Governance and Economic Management Assistance Programme (GEMAP), implemented from mid-2005 to 2007.[218]

DDR: Institutions and incentives

Within this socio-political context, the United States and the European Union played a direct role in DDR and SSR. The NCDDRR managed Liberia's DDR programme, and a joint implementation unit (JIU) included staff from the UN mission (UNMIL) and UNDP. The international community provided over 90 per cent of the total US$133 million spent on DDR in Liberia.[219] Modelled after Sierra Leone's DDR programme, a national commission was established to coordinate efforts between international and local actors.[220] The NTGL appointed Moses Jarbo (who was previously linked with LURD) as head of the NCDDRR.[221] Initially, international donor community representatives from UNMIL, ECOWAS, the European Community and the United States dominated the NCDDRR, which was to serve as both a policy (through the Policy Committee[222]) and a managerial/supervisory body. Approximately 400 Liberians staffed the NCDDRR.[223]

The responsibility for implementing the DDR programme rested within the authority of UNMIL's JIU, which reported directly to the deputy SRSG[224] and was primarily responsible for day-to-day implementation. Coordination and information sharing were facilitated through the programme and policy adviser (a non-Liberian UNDP staff member transferred from Sierra Leone's NCDDR), who reported to the UNDP country director, who interfaced with Jarbo on implementation of the DDR programme. UNMIL agreed to provide funding for Jarbo's office to support collaboration with the programme and policy adviser. The UN initially excluded the NTGL and the warring factions from this unit.[225]

TCCs comprising UNMIL commanders and members of the three warring factions were established to address implementation issues on the ground. Coordination and implementation support for the DDR programme was provided by UNDP, which reported to the project board. Additionally, a technical working group was created, chaired by an NCDDRR official and comprising specialists from UNMIL's reintegration, rehabilitation and recovery section, UNDP and the International Labour Organization.[226]

After order was re-established in Monrovia in late December, the UN authorities began to take the views of senior and junior commanders from the warring factions more seriously. A plan was negotiated with the factions' leaders to integrate some junior commanders into the NCDDRR to implement a national disarmament programme. This led in early 2004 to the NCDDRR hiring 16 junior commanders from each of the three factions (known as the "48 Generals") to assist UNMIL to implement disarmament. Their task was to convince, cajole and otherwise disarm all three factions in a systematic manner.[227] Additionally, this arrangement allowed time for the UN peacekeeping force to deploy gradually to some areas outside Monrovia before rolling out the nationwide DDR programme.

The overall management of DDR did not change significantly, since UNDP maintained leadership over the Multi-Donor Trust Fund, which financed the programme.[228] In May 2004 NCDDRR head Moses Jarbo complained to the deputy SRSG (Abou Moussa) that UN and international actors failed to include and consult members of the NTGL. Following a dispute between Jarbo and Moussa, the deputy SRSG for humanitarian affairs stepped in to lead UNMIL's efforts.[229] This created greater space for more governmental input through the integration of Liberian line ministries and members from the private sector and chamber of commerce into the NCDDR.

The disarmament programme resumed in early April 2004, backed by significant material resources from the UN.[230] With the help of junior commanders, UNMIL deployed to the different territories formerly controlled by LURD, the government and MODEL to negotiate with units throughout the country. Overall, the integration of the "48 Generals" had a positive impact in the implementation of DDR: relying heavily on the "Generals", an estimated 60 per cent of weapons were collected by November 2004 when the disarmament process came to a close. One of the problems was that many of the armaments were transferred across the borders to Guinea and Côte d'Ivoire.[231] Programmatically, the results of the DDR programme in Liberia were decidedly mixed,[232] and 102,193 Liberians participated, as compared to the initial estimates of 40,000 combatants.[233]

As one example of powerful incentives to exploit the international intervention, there was a proliferation of local community organizations in response to UN reintegration contracts.[234] Hundreds of local non-governmental organizations (NGOs) and community-based organizations were set up in Sierra Leone and Liberia to access resources from the international community's DDR programme.[235] The majority of these NGOs had little interest in establishing credible programmes and the UN project appraisal committee failed to use stringent standardized measures to ensure quality control, especially in terms of training that was offered.[236] As a result, the training that ex-combatants received fell well below local standards.[237] This contributed to considerable fraud and undermined the legitimacy of the DDR training programmes.

The second part of the puzzle was to fill the political vacuum by restoring a legitimate central state authority during the transition and laying foundations for democratic governance. An exploration of sectoral reforms in the security sector will shed some light on whether and to what extent some foundational basis of legitimate democratic governance based on respect for the rule of law and accountability was established.

SSR, democratic governance and state consolidation

The first two years of the transition were merely a holding pattern in an effort to "establish order and security" in preparation for the October 2005 elections. Given the weakness of central state authority during the first two years of the transition, the short-term priorities emphasized subsectoral components of SSR. Due to the above-outlined nature of the conflict and transition, police and defence reform were concentrated on so as to lay some initial foundations for a more "efficient, effective and accountable"[238] Liberian security sector. Thus the "first-order" priorities concerned specifically the police and military dimensions of SSR, involving the post-war Liberian National Police (LNP) restructured by the UN and the new national Armed Forces of Liberia (AFL) supported by the United States. The medium-term goals associated with holistic SSR and linked to national security governance and policy-making for both security and justice-providing institutions and management and oversight actors were left unaddressed until after a new democratically elected government came to power in 2005–2006.

The US government became the largest donor to the Liberian SSR intervention, contributing over US$220 million towards military reform.[239] UNMIL assumed a key security role and a lead role in reconstituting the LNP. The existing Liberian police force and its various ancillary units – including the notorious Anti-Terrorist Unit and the Special Security Services – from the former Taylor regime were viewed as ineffective, predatory and in need of substantive tear-down and reform. Donors sought to neutralize individuals from the former regime in the context of the DDR/SSR interventions.

DDR–SSR links

DDR and police reform
Instead of implementing holistic subsectoral SSR in the police aimed at enhancing good governance and establishing the rule of law and accountability, the early reform efforts led by the UN CivPol unit and commenced in December 2003 were implemented in an *ad hoc* manner to reconstitute an interim Liberian

police force to resume basic operational tasks.[240] The CivPol commander decided to retain some of the existing police officers from the previous regime to assist the UN forces to provide internal security until a proper Liberian police force could be established.[241] This decision was informed by practical constraints on the ground, particularly by the fact that UNMIL lacked authority and a mandate to arrest criminals; the embryonic reconstituted force, called the Liberian National Police, conducted joint crime prevention patrols alongside UN CivPol units for the month of December 2003.[242] Approximately 5,000 former LNP were reregistered in the LNP by early January 2004.[243] In an effort to neutralize the old Taylor regime, the vast majority of former police and intelligence officers were sidelined from playing any meaningful role during this period. As part of this broader attempt to shift power in favour of the NTGL, UNMIL took action in 2004 to demobilize approximately 3,000 former LNP, some 870 Special Security Services bodyguards and the entire Anti-Terrorist Unit.[244] A separate disarmament process for state security forces was implemented under the civilian DDR programme, financed by the Multi-Donor Trust Fund managed by UNDP.[245]

In contrast to the earlier *ad hoc* reforms, UNMIL engaged in foundational SSR tasks such as developing a civilian police training programme. After the NTGL was inaugurated in early January 2004, UNMIL police officers and the government of Liberia collaborated on a vetting and screening programme for initiating LNP recruitment. The NTGL was dependent on UNMIL to provide resources for these efforts, including setting up training plans at the National Police Academy and addressing logistical challenges.[246] UNMIL/CivPol set a new policy on recruitment in line with African standards, implemented a basic aptitude test and aimed to train a total of 3,500 police officers by June 2007.[247]

The LNP restructuring process failed to develop non-partisan local contacts that could provide intelligence on the backgrounds of recruits. UNMIL was thus unable to conduct extensive background checks on new LNP personnel and the screening process was limited to interviews with NGOs and community-based organizations, as opposed to collecting information from the local communities.[248] The CivPol-led vetting process resulted in a low rejection rate of 10 per cent.[249] Many high-school dropouts entered the new police force as a result. The slow deployment of UNMIL military troops, an unstable power-sharing government and poor initial planning for DDR contributed to a precarious security environment during the transition.

DDR and defence reform

The defence sector featured as a core component part of the Liberian SSR programme. As one of the primary good governance goals of comprehensive SSR, defence sector reform aims "to establish institutions that are well-led, honest, impartial, regarded as legitimate by the population at large, and committed to protecting and serving the entire population under the rule of law and with respect to human rights".[250] The Liberian defence reform programme focused on training and mentoring newly recruited civilians to staff the national Defence Ministry. As part of the wider SSR intervention, national security legislation was drafted and promulgated later in the process, after 2007.[251]

The warring factions had reached a consensus during the Accra peace talks to outsource the SSR component of AFL reform to the US government.[252] In 2004, when the bulk of the UN-led disarmament and demobilization phases were implemented, some limited gains were achieved in reform of the AFL.[253] While the NTGL had little incentive to develop the national security framework necessary for good governance of the security sector, and specifically the armed forces, the transitional MOD engaged in some preliminary defence reforms. Since little implementation took place, there were fewer opportunities to sequence DDR with AFL reform. The process was held up in part due to a lack of resources and because the US government did not make any decisions on how to handle its responsibilities for AFL reform until 2004–2005. During a meeting at the Pentagon in mid-2004, the US government offered to retrain and re-equip the army and finance the severance packages as long as the Liberian authorities took full responsibility for their own demobilization process.[254] However, the US government was legally prevented from covering the severance pay for retiring soldiers in a country that lacked a democratically elected government. Liberian and US defence officials discussed recruitment policies and proposals related to the new and appropriately sized army.[255]

In early 2004 discussions took place with the NTGL Ministry of National Defence[256] on how to handle proposals for the defence component of SSR. Despite some initial internal bickering between members of the Defence Advisory Committee (DAC) in the ministry, the group was able to agree on a plan to develop a new national army it called the Liberian National Defence Force, comprising 6,500 personnel.[257] The plan also called for building an army infantry brigade, the Air Reconnaissance Unit, the Liberian National Coast Guard and a reserve unit. Defence Minister Daniel Chea presented the proposal to retain a core group of 50–100 senior officers to form the foundation for the new force. The Liberian plan was justified on the grounds that a military cannot be built from scratch and had to be re-established based on what already existed.[258]

Since at the time the US Department of Defense (DoD) was preoccupied with its intense military engagements in Afghanistan and Iraq, the US Department of State (DoS) made the decision to outsource its commitments to reform the AFL to two US-based private security companies, DynCorp and Pacific Architects and Engineers (PAE).[259] The DoS would coordinate US efforts, while DynCorp and PAE would take charge of implementing these sectoral reforms.[260]

In mid-May 2004 a team of DoD officials and personnel from the contractors was deployed to Liberia for a 10-day assessment mission.[261] The team ignored the previous DAC Liberian plan and proposed its own option of creating a 4,020-person AFL force, including a 412-strong combat engineer battalion. Curiously, the US assessment team envisioned the need to conduct tasks such as demining, constructing field fortifications and digging tank traps when mines and tanks were completely absent.[262]

In late October 2004 DynCorp was awarded the contract for restructuring the AFL as part of defence reform.[263] DynCorp and PAE failed to engage with Liberian defence officials in an open and transparent manner. Their employees reported directly to DoS staff through the US embassy in Monrovia and were insulated from being held accountable to the Liberian defence minister. In May 2005, when Liberia was struggling to roll out its reintegration programme, the US government appointed Ambassador Donald Booth to manage and oversee US peacebuilding activities in Liberia. Liberian defence officials from the NTGL were unable to implement basic statebuilding tasks, including completing the demobilization of existing AFL personnel.[264] This led the DoS to conclude an MOU with the chair of the NTGL in an effort to clarify engagement.

The MOU became a framework to guide Liberia's defence reform process. The involvement of the US ambassador and US defence attaché gave much-needed legitimacy to the US programme. The contract stipulated that the demobilization of the old AFL was the primary responsibility of the NTGL.[265] The United States insisted on Liberia completing the demobilization of the AFL before it could initiate its defence reform assistance. Within the DAC, Defence Minister Daniel Chea and Internal Affairs Minister Blamo Nelson designed and implemented a redocumentation process for the AFL in 2004. The DAC relied on old Ministry of National Defence rudimentary records of pay stubs and recovered files from the MOD G1 section. The DAC classified soldiers into two broad categories: AFL personnel recruited by the governments of Doe and Taylor since 1990, who would be demobilized; and the pre-1980 soldiers, who would be "honourably retired".[266] The process became politicized when Krahn tribe elements in the AFL decided to inflate the number of personnel in the army so as to receive a greater amount of the severance packages.[267] According to informants from the DAC, the majority of the AFL were to be demobilized, reducing the AFL's size from some 13,000–14,000 soldiers and officers to about 300 officers.[268] These 300 senior officers would form the core of a new army comprising some 4,000 troops.

However, the existing Liberian Ministry of National Defence's perceived mismanagement of the demobilization process created an opportunity for DynCorp to take over some other policy-making functions. First, the Liberian proposal was discarded in favour of a US plan to disband the entire army. This decision was controversial among military officers, but was pushed through and approved by the interim chair of the NTGL with the signing into law of Special Executive Order #5 on 15 May 2005.[269] Senior officers in the AFL and some NTGL officials protested the decision, viewing it as unconstitutional and illegal.[270] Despite protests from the army, full demobilization of the AFL was implemented with strong US and international backing.

The MOU committed the United States to assisting the Liberian authorities to demobilize the existing military, followed by a rigorous recruitment and vetting process. After these components were completed, US military assistance focused on reforms in the defence sector aimed at enhancing the basic effectiveness and professionalization of the armed forces through modernization and train-and-equip elements, and providing infrastructural aid to outfit the new force. DynCorp trainers arrived in Monrovia in mid-2005, surprised to find that demobilization had not been completed. DynCorp was forced to complete the bulk of the demobilization of nearly 13,000 soldiers and officers and about 400 Defence Ministry staff.[271]

A provision in the MOU agreed the establishment of a Liberian–US Joint Defense Advisory Committee (JDAC) that was charged with formulating policy for the SSR programme and (jointly) overseeing its administration/implementation. The JDAC included two statutory members: the Liberian minister of national defence and a "US senior military representative", notably the chief of the US Office of Defense Cooperation in Liberia (filled by the defence attaché at the US embassy in Monrovia).[272] The US embassy (through Ambassador Donald Booth) maintained a strong and active role in providing political leadership on the ground. However, in practice the United States maintained autonomous influence over decision-making processes, and in many cases sidelined Liberia's NTGL defence officials from playing much of an administration and oversight role.[273] US defence officials made an executive decision to establish a 2,000-strong national army, based on their understanding of Liberia's budgetary constraints, instead of consulting local experts or conducting a comprehensive threat assessment.[274]

Due to the significant challenges and delays in completing the demobilization, the US-led recruitment and vetting process could not commence until 2006. DynCorp instructors sat idle in Monrovia for the latter half of 2005 and most of 2006.[275] During this time DynCorp's consultants continued to be paid, draining the SSR project budget.

At this time, the UN and the NTGL were muddling through the reintegration component of the DDR programme. DynCorp staff designed and implemented a rigorous vetting and screening process for the AFL that kicked off on 18 January 2006, two days after President Ellen Johnson-Sirleaf was inaugurated in office. The first batch of 106 soldiers commenced their basic entry-level training in May 2006, and this group subsequently graduated in November of the same year.

The dysfunction within the NTGL resulted in a delayed national consensus for handling the AFL reform. Although the Liberian transitional defence officials drafted their own plan for rebuilding the AFL, the general incompetence within the NTGL and a lack of economic capacity prevented effective implementation. When the new democratically elected government of Johnson-Sirleaf came to power in 2006, Liberian authorities outsourced many key policy-making tasks to external actors.[276] The US government imposed its own plan for handling AFL reform and maximized its autonomy from Liberian stakeholders. As a result, the DDR programme and early sectoral SSR efforts of the AFL were implemented independently of each other.

Main findings on the DDR–SSR relationship

Liberia lacked a stable political settlement with an interest in creating a sufficiently strong central state during the two-year transitional government. The political leaders from the former factions lacked incentives to implement countrywide disarmament, so peacebuilders had to rely more on the remaining command structures of the three factions to restore order following the failed UN disarmament process in December, and later to overcome coordination and information deficiencies related to DDR. Liberia's immediate transition suggests that the warring factions' residual organizational capacity for collective action may have been greater than that of the central state, at least in terms of the capacity of the "48 Generals" to "get things done". In the absence of a central state authority, the hierarchical structures of irregular armed groups were an important and relatively efficient resource for controlling the ex-combatants.[277] Additionally, UNMIL's extensive peacekeeping presence was a necessary but insufficient step to fill the power vacuum left after the integration of the factions in government and disarmament of their commanders and lower ranks. UNMIL authorities made the mistake of assuming that integrating the senior leaders into the NTGL would be sufficient to secure buy-in from the factions, which destabilized the security situation in Monrovia in late 2003. The Liberian transition underscores the dangers of imposing blueprint logics on very different socio-political contexts and misreading local power dynamics. UNMIL was ill prepared to fill the vacuum from the mobilized warring factions, which contributed to a breakdown in the disarmament process in early December 2003.[278] The two-year transition period reduced the time horizon for the integrated political leaders to concentrate on rent-seeking within the state. There were fewer incentives for them to support a well-ordered disarmament process. The UN's assumption that this was a necessary and sufficient condition to implement disarmament was naïve. The junior commanders excluded from political or military positions had to be integrated into the DDR process to overcome information and coordination challenges. In short, factional buy-in from senior leadership was a necessary but insufficient condition for disarmament.

In hindsight, there were (missed) opportunities for linking DDR and SSR. For instance, considering it had already been decided that irregular combatants would not be permitted to integrate into the army, and given the nature of the precarious NTGL, one strategy could have involved some special combatant programme for the remaining senior and mid-rank commanders not part of the NTGL who acted as gatekeepers to the rank and file. The senior and junior (mid-rank) commanders have varying degrees of power to disrupt state restoration processes in post-civil-war politics, based on their continued access to the means of violence (arms and ammunition) and their networks for remobilization. DDR and SSR share a common statebuilding objective to neutralize these actors through inducement, socialization or coercion. Mediators must possess good intelligence on the relative power of commanders, and where their potential loyalties with powerful figures may lie.

Three main structural factors inhibited DDR–SSR linkages from developing on the ground. First, the absence of a unified state underpinned by a stable political settlement prevented effective implementation of DDR and SSR policies (as a collective action problem). When the transitional government was formed, factions splintered into separate units based on new alliances and loyalties. When Liberian authorities in the MOD engaged in policy-making processes (i.e. the Liberian plan to retain a core group of officers from the army), their ideas were eventually discarded in favour of US plans.[279] The NTGL seemed uninterested in executing vital statebuilding tasks, preferring instead to maximize rent-seeking opportunities and pass the burden of statebuilding on to external donors. Since external actors were required to step in to perform major statebuilding roles (through GEMAP and military restructuring), it would appear that more direct involvement in other areas, including defence reform, was required. These factors contributed to more top-down, externally driven DDR and SSR programmes, characterized by minimal Liberian input in national policy-making processes.

Second, US-led military reform advisers seemed to operate in silos, which also explains the lack of mechanisms to link up with the NCDDRR. On the ground, DynCorp and PAE preferred to conduct their work autonomously from Liberian stakeholders. The only real evidence of a link established during the implementation phase was when DynCorp consultants requested access to the NCDDRR's database on ex-combatants. Senior staff in the NCDDRR accepted the request and provided the database to DynCorp without delay; it was used to verify the identity of individuals under consideration for employment in the new AFL, and to a more limited extent in the Liberian national security apparatus.

Lastly, timing and sequencing appear to be critical factors in an overall disjointed DDR–SSR approach. DDR was implemented in the context of a transitional government before substantive SSR commenced, and well before national security policy development became a priority.

Conclusion

As existing literature on DDR and SSR presumes the existence of an already consolidated state, this paper seeks to introduce the assumption that linking DDR and SSR effectively in practice requires taking the post-conflict peacebuilding and statebuilding context into consideration. In particular, it argues that the processes of restoring the state as the sole authority capable of legitimately using force and legitimizing the state both affect the programming and implementation of DDR and SSR. Based on statebuilding literature, it is evident that the nature of the conflict and how it ends, the nature and interests of the central state authority, the central state's relative strength *vis-à-vis* the relative influence of international actors, and local capacities for change affect the success of DDR and SSR in such transitions. The paper proposes that DDR and SSR should be regarded as two distinct processes occurring at concurrent or different periods in time with overlapping objectives in a war-to-peace transition. Linking DDR with SSR is especially important in the context of enhancing democratic governance, which can facilitate DDR. This is evidenced in Sierra Leone, where the state was first restored and subsequently reformed before the management of arms could be addressed.

While it is impossible to generalize the findings of the comparative analysis of relatively older West African case studies involving externally assisted statebuilding, the cases suggest that local context can potentially shape the outcome of these interventions.[280] As this paper demonstrates, existing research has overemphasized supply-side considerations in DDR–SSR programming. The evidence provides a stepping-stone for future studies focusing on linking DDR and SSR in post-conflict environments by raising the important issue of demand-side considerations in war-to-peace transtitions, which can facilitate or spoil DDR–SSR programming. Since this contains a comparative analysis of only two cases, it is imperative to include a larger number and broader range of countries in future empirical research on this topic. Despite their weak explanatory power, the cases of Sierra Leone and Liberia nevertheless provide lessons learned that can have implications for other cases in post-conflict contexts and inform future studies.

In *Sierra Leone* the post-conflict state engaged in national policy-making related to DDR and SSR. The fundamental reason for this is that the Kabbah state had an interest in consolidating its power and restoring its authority in society, and saw some elements of DDR and SSR as opportunities to achieve these goals. This convergence of interests between national politicians and external donors occurred within the context of a distinct shift in power in favour of the government in mid-2000 that created the conditions for effective implementation of the Lomé accord. The DDR programme sponsored by the UN and World Bank laid the ground for a national disarmament programme. External actors supported the Kabbah state to overcome challenges related to coordination and collective action to follow up this UN disarmament with two subsequent community disarmament programmes of its own. These programmes collectively allowed the central government to restore itself as the sole political authority capable of legitimately using force. British advisers were able to reinforce the shift in power for the state by implementing SSR, particularly in the police, military and national security architecture. These efforts were embraced largely because the Kabbah state wanted to legitimize itself in the eyes of international donors. The UK-led police reform allowed a comprehensive arms reduction process to occur, while the development of a system for arms licensing/registration was led by UNDP. The government could, however, sideline certain sensitive aspects of this process through its own domestic national processes.

In *Liberia* a defining characteristic of the early transition process was the fact that the warring factions became the state. The Accra peace accord resulted in an unstable and inefficient political settlement (or power-sharing arrangement) underpinning state power, which limited the possibilities for national policy-making on DDR and SSR-related tasks. Additionally, there were no national security frameworks in place to guide DDR and AFL/LNP reform. The possibility of linking DDR and SSR tasks was additionally hampered by the fact that the US government's approach to military reform was not conducive to significant cooperation and collaboration with non-US entities. The US SSR practitioners who implemented military reform preferred to work on their own terms with minimal Liberian involvement and "buy-in", while UNMIL and UNDP operated mostly in isolation during DDR-related activities. In other words, UN DDR practitioners and SSR staff seemed to operate as if they were in silos, in isolation from one another. This suggests that the nature of a state's authority after the end of a war matters significantly for possible DDR–SSR synergies.

In the power-sharing context of Liberia, international actors were far less successful in filling the vacuum of central state authority than in Sierra Leone. This failure negatively impacted on other areas of the reconstruction process, as ex-combatants (some of whom remained linked to the NTGL authorities) became the most likely group to fill these institutional vacuums to exploit the international intervention. In some instances, some local capacities were overlooked or sidelined. Thus the nature of the state authority in post-conflict contexts is a critical variable for the DDR–SSR nexus, and conditions what degree of integration is feasible.

The SSR agenda in both countries was linked to broader practices to shape preferences of actors within the state and the security sector, and to alter incentive structures to inculcate the principles of accountability, transparency and participatory decision-making into security institutions in the developing world.[281] Despite SSR's perceived infringement of sovereignty, the Kabbah state in *Sierra Leone* embraced the SSR concept, at least initially. The president himself requested outside assistance, appointed expatriate police and military officers as national security advisers and allowed external advisers to assume key roles in the development of SSR policies and strategies. There were obvious political benefits in embracing some dimensions of SSR, at least in the short term, to gain international legitimacy and capitalize on gains made during the transition process to consolidate domestic power. In *Liberia* members of the transitional government were more interested in rent-seeking opportunities, and due to their short time horizon had fewer incentives to support far-reaching measures that promoted accountability and transparency.

There is no standard formula for integrating DDR and SSR in practice, since it assumes a sufficient degree of political commitment on the part of lead external donors to operationalize synergies in practice (and problematically assumes that these outside actors know what is "best" for recipient countries). This paper demonstrates that operationalizing DDR–SSR links also largely depend a great deal on the local power relations in a given post-war context, the nature of central state authority and whether there is a sufficient convergence of interests. The role that DDR and SSR can play in this regard can perhaps be enhanced if they are complemented by a range of other instruments that can secure a stable distribution of political power for a central authority, and if those efforts are matched by initiatives to ensure that the state is sufficiently concerned about its own legitimacy to protect all its citizens from violence.

Regarding the central research question of this paper – under what conditions DDR and SSR programmes can be linked in practice – the findings suggest that international actors may be more likely to integrate DDR and SSR when there is a stable political settlement underlying state authority and the power holders view elements of DDR and SSR as strategies to consolidate their power and/or enhance their domestic/international legitimacy. The actual form that this DDR–SSR relationship will take is likely to depend on power relations between the host state and international actors.

The case studies show that a number of mechanisms were established to link DDR and SSR in practice. In *Sierra Leone* the British-led IMATT SSR process developed some programmatic links with certain elements of the DDR programmes. These mechanisms were established mostly to facilitate information sharing and collaboration on logistics to ensure a smoother transfer of combatants to the military and civilian reintegration programmes. One finding from the case study suggests a direct link between the degree of external commitment and involvement in a transition process and prospects for planning for DDR–SSR synergies. British officials had the distinct advantage of embedding a team of civilians in the MOD in Sierra Leone to carry out upstream planning on SSR-related policies in 1998–1999. This provided an opportunity to plan before the British took direct control of more ambitious reform processes once political conditions allowed. In *Liberia* the only real evidence of a practical link between DDR and SSR was a communication link established by DynCorp SSR officials with senior Liberian staff in the NCDDRR to access information from its database to help with the vetting/screening process for the AFL. This evidence can be a basis for further research into other case studies.

At the programmatic level, DDR databases were a useful resource for the investigative work of SSR practitioners involved in vetting and screening exercises, particularly for army recruits.[282] This may be particularly important in underdeveloped contexts where information on recruits is scarce and the cost of collecting intelligence is high. Depending on the degree of political interference in state security forces, SSR programmes may involve groundwork for establishing new basic rules for recruitment and selection criteria, including deciding whether to integrate ex-combatants into the armed forces. The 2009 IDDRS module states that "clear criteria should be established to ensure that individuals with inappropriate backgrounds or training are not re-deployed within the security sector".[283] Basic information such as demographics on individual combatants collected during demobilization can be a useful resource to aid in the identification of appropriate personnel in support of internationally acceptable vetting processes. From this perspective, demobilization can been seen as a "filtering process" that supports SSR-related decisions on whether a particular individual is suitable for official security duties.[284]

To conclude, DDR and SSR planners could rely on both deductive and inductive approaches to the study of power relations within post-conflict states and between social forces engaged in struggles for control of state power, which could also be a focus of future empirical studies on this topic. This framework should emphasize several elements: the political and economic interests of the most powerful actors involved; how likely specific measures are to destabilize the system, and who are the likely political losers; the extent to which DDR and SSR practices can place constraints on the exercise of power by powerful actors; and how DDR and SSR activities are used instrumentally by the state to pursue its political interests.

Notes

1 Andy Knight, "Linking DDR and SSR in post-conflict peacebuilding in Africa: An overview", *African Journal of Political Science and International Relations*, Vol. 4, No. 1 (2010), pp. 29–54; Alan Bryden and Vincenza Scherrer (eds), *Disarmament, Demobilization and Reintegration and Security Sector Reform* (Munster: LIT Verlag, 2012); Mark Sedra (ed.), *The Future of Security Sector Reform* (Waterloo, ON: CIGI, 2010).

2 United Nations, "Integrated DDR standards. Module 6.10: DDR and security sector reform", New York, 2009, http://issat.dcaf.ch/content/download/3093/26375/file/UN%20 IDDRS%20DDR%20and%20SSR.pdf; OECD-DAC, *OECD-DAC Handbook on Security System Reform: Supporting Security and Justice* (Paris: OECD, 2007), pp. 108–109.

3 Bryden and Scherrer, note 1 above; Michael Miklaucic and Melanne A. Civic, *Monopoly of Force: The Nexus of DDR and SSR* (Washington, DC: National Defense University Press, 2011); Knight, note 1 above; Michael Brzoska, "Embedding DDR programmes in security sector reconstruction", in Alan Bryden and Heiner Hänggi (eds), *Security Governance in Post-Conflict Peacebuilding* (London: DCAF/Transaction Publishers, 2005).

4 Hugo de Vries and Erwin van Veen, "Living apart together? On the difficult linkage between DDR and SSR in post-conflict environments", Clingendael Conflict Research Unit Policy Brief 15, The Hague, October 2010.

5 See for instance UN best practices and "lessons learned" documents, such as United Nations, note 2 above.

6 Joanna Spear, "The disarmament and demobilization of warring factions in the aftermath of civil wars: Key implementation issues", *Civil Wars*, Vol. 2, No. 2 (1999), pp. 1–22.

7 While there is no consensus definition of statebuilding, Paris and Sisk define it as a "sub-component of peacebuilding" that is concerned with "the strengthening or construction of legitimate governmental institutions in countries that are emerging from conflicts". Roland Paris and Timothy Sisk, *The Dilemmas of Statebuilding: Confronting the Contradictions of Postwar Peace Operations* (London: Routledge, 2009), p. 14.

8 William Zartman, *Collapsed States: The Disintegration and Restoration of Legitimate Authority* (Boulder, CO: Lynne Rienner, 1995); Peter Lassman and Ronald Speirs, *Weber: Political Writings* (Cambridge: Cambridge University Press, 1994), pp. 310–311.

9 Charles T. Call, *Constructing Justice and Security after War* (Washington, DC: US Institute of Peace Press, 2007), p. 7.

10 Timothy Donais (ed.), *Local Ownership and Security Sector Reform* (Munster: LIT Verlag, 2008); Alex de Waal, "Mission without end? Peacekeeping in the African political marketplace", *International Affairs*, Vol. 85, No. 1 (2009), pp. 99–113; D. Hendrickson and A. Karkoszka, "Security sector reform and donor policies", in Albrecht Schnabel and Hans-Georg Ehrhart (eds), *Security Sector Reform and Post-Conflict Peacebuilding* (Tokyo: United Nations University Press, 2005).

11 Tony Addison, "Reconstruction from war in Africa: Communities, entrepreneurs, and states", Discussion Paper No. 2001/18, UNO/WIDER, Helsinki, 2001.

12 Duncan Barley, "Rebuilding Afghanistan's security forces: Security sector reform in contested state-Building", *RUSI Journal*, Vol. 153, No. 3 (2008), p. 52. It is not explicitly stated *why* these cases were relatively more "benign", however.

13 For a comprehensive history of contemporary DDR see Robert Muggah, *Security and Post-Conflict Reconstruction: Dealing with Fighters in the Aftermath of War* (London: Routledge, 2009).

14 Lena Sundh and Jens Samuelsson Schjørlien (eds), "Stockholm Initiative on Disarmament, Demobilization and Reintegration (SIDDR): Final report", Swedish Ministry for Foreign Affairs, Stockholm, 2006, p. 14.

15 Alcira Kreimer, "The World Bank's experience with post-conflict reconstruction", World Bank, Washington, DC, 1998, https://ieg.worldbankgroup.org/Data/reports/postcon.pdf.

16 United Nations, "Second generation DDR", 2010, www.un.org/en/peacekeeping/documents/2GDDR_ENG_WITH_COVER.pdf, p. 25; Denise Garcia, *Small Arms and Security: New Emerging International Norms* (London: Routledge, 2006).

17 UN General Assembly, "Note by the Secretary-General on administrative and budgetary aspects of the financing of UN peacekeeping operations", 24 May 2005, UN Doc. A/C.5/59/31.

18 United Nations, note 2 above, p. 18.

19 UN General Assembly, note 17 above.

20 United Nations, note 2 above.

21 Paul Collier, "Demobilization and insecurity: A study in the economics of the transition from war to peace", *Journal of International Development*, Vol. 6, No. 3 (1994), pp. 343–351.

22 United Nations, note 2 above.

23 Robert Muggah and Nat Colletta, "Rethinking post-war security promotion", *Journal of Security Sector Management*, Vol. 7, No. 1 (2009), p. 1.

24 Muggah, note 13 above.

25 Knight, note 1 above.

26 Bryden and Scherrer, note 1 above, p. 6.

27 Nicole Ball, "The evolution of the security sector reform agenda", in Sedra, note 1 above, p. 29; Hendrickson and Karkoszka, note 10 above, p. 176.

28 The degree to which specific national authorities embrace these post-conflict reforms and allow for a role for international actors varies depending on the context.

29 Kofi Annan, "Peace and development – One struggle, two fronts", address of the UN Secretary-General to World Bank staff, 19 October 1999, http://reliefweb.int/report/afghanistan/united-nations-secretary-general-kofi-annan-address-world-bank-staff-peace-and.

30 For a comprehensive list of all the monitoring institutions and organizations see Dylan Hendrickson and Adrezj Karkoszka, "The challenges of security sector reform", in *SIPRI Yearbook 2002: Armaments, Disarmament and International Security* (Stockholm: SIPRI, 2002), www.sipri.org/yearbook/2002/files/SIPRIYB0204.pdf, p. 181.

31 Ibid., p. 180.

32 Nicole Ball and Dylan Hendrickson, "Trends in security sector reform (SSR): Policy, practice and research", CSDG Papers Number 20, King's College, London, March 2009, www.securityanddevelopment.org/www.securityanddevelopment.org/pdf/CSDG%20Paper%2020.pdf, pp. 14–24; Michael Brzoska, "Development donors and the concept of security sector reform", Occasional Paper 4, DCAF, Geneva, 2003, pp. 33–36.

33 SSR is considered as a policy process aimed at enhancing security sector governance. See DCAF's SSR Backgrounders for these distinctions, http://ssrbackgrounders.org.

34 OECD-DAC, note 2 above.

35 Ibid., p. 105.

36 United Nations, "Securing peace and development: The role of the United Nations in supporting security sector reform", report of the Secretary-General, 2008, UN Doc. A/62/659-S/2008/39. See Ministry of Foreign Affairs of the Slovak Republic, "Developing

a security sector reform concept for the United Nations", proceedings of expert workshop, Bratislava, 7 July 2006, www.securitycouncilreport.org/atf/cf/%7B65BFCF9B-6D27-4E9C-8CD3-CF6E4FF96FF9%7D/SSR%204%20Developing.pdf, p. 5.

37 United Nations, ibid., para. 17.

38 Since the UN Charter prohibits intervention in the domestic political and security affairs of its member states, the UN is restricted to tasks that support the host state's own national initiatives. The UN's work is therefore focused on improving the capacity of member states to comply with international norms.

39 UN Security Council, "Security sector reform in post-conflict states critical to consolidating peace, report needed aimed at improving UN effectiveness, Security Council says", press release, 20 February 2007, UN Doc. SC/8958.

40 See Call, note 9 above, p. 405.

41 See the arguments of Cuba and Egypt in the Security Council's discussions on the organization's role in SSR. UN Security Council, "The maintenance of international peace and security: Role of the Security Council in supporting security sector reform", Repertoire of the Practice of the Security Council, 2004–2007, www.un.org/en/sc/repertoire/2004-2007/Chapter%208/Thematic/04-07_8_SC%20role%20in%20 supporting%20security%20sector%20reform.pdf, p. 785.

42 Max Weber, "Politics as vocation", in *Max Weber: Essays in Sociology* (New York: Oxford University Press, 1968), pp. 77–128.

43 OECD-DAC, *Security Sector Reform and Governance*, DAC Guidelines and Reference Series (Paris: OECD, 2005), p. 64.

44 Alan Bryden and Heiner Hänggi (eds), *Security Governance in Post-Conflict Peacebuilding* (London: DCAF/Transaction Publishers, 2005).

45 Donais, note 10 above, p. 45.

46 While post-conflict contexts vary, there is a high likelihood that under such conditions the remaining state authority will be based on personal loyalty, with little or no separation between the "private" and "official" spheres (or what some scholars characterize as the patrimonial structure). See for instance Patrick Chabol and Jean-Pascal Daloz, *Africa Works: Disorder as Political Instrument* (Bloomington, IN: Indiana University Press, 1999).

47 Bryden and Scherrer, note 1 above, p. 9.

48 Ibid.

49 Ibid, p. 10

50 There is a lively debate ongoing within the UN about whether DDR is indeed a subcomponent of SSR (author's conversation with UN staff). See also Bryden and Hänggi, note 44 above, p. 33; Alan Bryden, "Pushing pieces around the chessboard or changing the game? DDR, SSR and the security–development nexus", in Albrecht Schnabel and Vanessa Farr (eds), *Back to the Roots: Security Sector Reform and Development* (Munster: LIT Verlag, 2012), p. 205.

51 Bryden, note 50 above, p. 205.

52 The UN IAWG-DDR created a subgroup during the development of the DDR–SSR module for the IDDRS, which was intended to foster critical linkages with SSR. This module was one of the first attempts to flesh out the policy synergies and linkages between DDR and SSR.

53 de Vries and van Veen, note 4 above.

54 Knight, note 1 above, p. 41.

55 Roy Licklider (ed.) *New Armies from Old: Merging Competing Military Forces after Civil War* (Washington, DC: Georgetown University Press, 2014).

56 K. Glassmyer and N. Sambanis, "Rebel–military integration and civil war termination", *Journal of Peace Research*, Vol. 45, No. 3 (2008), pp. 365–384.

57 United Nations, note 2 above.

58 Bryden and Scherrer, note 1 above; United Nations, "Integrated DDR standards. Module 3.30: National institutions for DDR", United Nations, New York, 2006.

59 Adrian Leftwich, *Developmental States, Effective States and Poverty Reduction: The Primacy of Politics* (Geneva: UNRISD, 2008).

60 Virginia Page Fortna, *Does Peacekeeping Work? Shaping Belligerents' Choices after Civil War* (Princeton, NJ: Princeton University Press, 2008), p. 94.

61 Research that connects disarmament with the local political economy has advanced knowledge on the challenges of implementing these tasks. Disarmament may be connected to broader efforts aimed at altering or disrupting incentive structures in a post-conflict society that sustain militarization as a viable economic strategy for some local actors. See Paul Collier, "Doing well out of war: An economic perspective", in Mats Berdal and David Malone (eds), *Greed and Grievance: Economic Agendas in Civil Wars* (Boulder, CO: Lynne Rienner, 2000); David Keen, "Incentives and disincentives for violence", in Mats Berdal and David Malone (eds), *Greed and Grievance: Economic Agendas in Civil Wars* (Boulder, CO: Lynne Rienner, 2000).

62 In the absence of this condition, disarmament may be dependent in part on broader international (UN Security Council) commitments to prevent transfers of arms and light weapons in volatile transitional contexts.

63 Mats Berdal, *Disarmament and Demobilization after Civil Wars: Arms, Soldiers and the Termination of Conflict*, Adelphi Paper No. 303 (London: Routledge, 1996).

64 These networks can be remobilized in a context where arms are not fully collected.

65 Reintegration assistance has been criticized for lacking quality training, sustainable funding and serious interest from donors. Macartan Humphreys and Jeremy M. Weinstein, "Demobilization and reintegration", *Journal of Conflict Resolution*, Vol. 51, No. 4 (2007), p. 531; Sundh and Schjørlien, note 14 above.

66 The UN refers to these as "special commander programmes". United Nations, note 16 above.

67 Paul Bonard and Yvon Conoir, "Evaluation of UNDP reintegration programmes: Final evaluation report", February 2013, UNDP, New York, p. 31.

68 United Nations, note 58 above. In this sense, scholars have urged that reintegration should be more effectively linked with economic development strategies. Knight, note 1 above.

69 Doyle and Sambanis have developed one of the most elaborate analytical and empirical frameworks on peacebuilding – a large-n cross-country study which compared over a hundred international peacebuilding efforts in civil-war-affected countries. Their findings emphasize three variables that jointly shape probabilities of peacebuilding success or failure at the aggregate level: international capacity (or commitment), local capacity, and residual animosity between previously warring factions. Mark Doyle and Nicholas Sambanis, "International peacebuilding: A theoretical and quantitative analysis", *American Political Science Review*, Vol. 94, No. 4 (2000), pp. 779–801; Mark Doyle and Nicholas Sambanis, *Making War and Building Peace* (Princeton, NJ: Princeton University Press, 2006).

70 Robert Harrison Wagner, "The causes of peace", in Roy Licklider (ed.), *Stopping the Killing: How Civil Wars End* (New York: New York University Press, 1993); Monica Duffy Toft, "Ending civil wars: A case for rebel victory?", *International Security*, Vol. 34, No. 4

(2010), pp. 7–36; Barbara F. Walter, "Designing transitions from civil war: Demobilization, democratization and commitments to peace", *International Security*, Vol. 24, No. 1 (1999), pp. 127–155; Jeremy Weinstein, "Autonomous recovery and international intervention in comparative perspective", Working Paper No. 57, Centre for Global Development, Washington, DC, April 2005.

71 Roy Licklider, "The consequences of negotiated settlements in civil wars, 1945–1993", *American Political Science Review*, Vol. 89, No. 3 (1995), p. 684.

72 There is a tendency for the international community to support hasty "quick-fix" resolutions that will immediately stop the fighting. Pierre Englebert and Dennis M. Tull, "Post-conflict resolution in Africa: Flawed ideas about failed states", *International Security*, Vol. 32, No. 1 (2008), p. 106.

73 Caroline Hartzell, "Institutionalizing peace: Power-sharing and post-civil war conflict", *American Journal of Political Science*, Vol. 47, No. 2 (2003), p. 318.

74 Weinstein, note 70 above; de Waal, note 10 above.

75 Toft, note 70 above; Monica Toft, *Securing the Peace: The Durable Settlement of Civil Wars* (Princeton, NJ: Princeton University Press, 2009); Licklider, note 71 above; Hartzell, note 73 above.

76 Weinstein, note 70 above.

77 Relative strength is defined in terms of political and military power (capital, accumulation of arms, fighting skills, degree of support from the civilian population), and military capabilities (their capacity to hold on to territory, and what "external" support they receive). Weinstein, note 70 above.

78 Jonathan Di John, "The concept, causes and consequences of failed states: A critical review of the literature and agenda for research with specific reference to sub-Saharan Africa", *European Journal of Development Research*, Vol. 22 (2010), pp. 10–30; OECD, *Supporting Statebuilding in Situations of Fragility and Conflict* (Paris: OECD, 2011); Berdal, note 63 above; Spear, note 6 above.

79 Andreas Wimmer, Lars-Erik Cederman and Brian Min, "Ethnic politics and armed conflict: A configurational analysis of a new global data set", *American Sociological Review*, Vol. 74, No. 2 (2009), p. 316.

80 Walter, note 70 above; Barbara F. Walter, *Committing to Peace: The Successful Settlement of Civil Wars* (Princeton, NJ: Princeton University Press, 2002), pp. 104–105. See also Doyle and Sambanis (2006), note 69 above.

81 Zartman, note 8 above, p. 269; Stephen Stedman, "Spoiler problems in peace processes", *International Security*, Vol. 22, No. 2 (1998), pp. 5–53.

82 Collective action problems are defined as pervasive dilemmas found where the pursuit of short-term, self-interested strategies leaves everyone worse off than other possible alternatives might. See Mancur Olson, *The Logic of Collective Action: Public Goods and the Theory of Groups*, 20th edn (Cambridge, MA: Harvard University Press, 2002); Elinor Ostrom, "A behavior approach to the rational choice theory of collective action", *American Political Science Review*, Vol. 92, No. 1 (1998), p. 1.

83 There is, however, a particular risk that this assistance will reduce incentives for the state to engage directly in this bargaining process with citizens. See Todd Moss, Gunilla Pettersson and Nicolas van de Walle, "An aid-institutions paradox?", Center for Global Development Working Paper, Washington, DC, 2006; Deborah Brautigam and Stephen Knack, "Foreign aid, institutions and governance in sub-Saharan Africa", *Economic Development and Cultural Change*, Vol. 52, No. 2 (2004), pp. 255–285.

84   Berdal, note 63 above.

85   Virgina Page Fortna talks about a shift in power between factions in post-intrastate conflict contexts, in which UN peacekeepers play a third-party role to shape the choices of belligerents. She draws on international relations theory on the balance of power to explain domestic power shifts. See Fortna, note 60 above, p. 83.

86   The costs of deploying coercion are higher than bargaining and are more difficult to sustain over the longer term. Robert Bates, *When Things Fell Apart: State Failure in Late-Century Africa* (Cambridge: University of Cambridge Press, 2008).

87   Di John, note 78 above.

88   Albrecht Schnabel and Hans Born, "Security sector reform: Narrowing the gap between theory and practice", DCAF, Geneva, 2011, www.dcaf.ch/Publications/Security-Sector-Reform-Narrowing-the-Gap-between-Theory-and-Practice, p. 6.

89   Doyle and Sambanis (2006), note 69 above.

90   The crucial point is that these two sources of funding are problematic because governments that are dependent on aid and rents from resources have fewer incentives to engage directly with their citizens. Mick Moore, "Political underdevelopment: What causes 'bad governance'?", *Public Management Review*, Vol. 3, No. 3 (2001), p. 385.

91   Doyle and Sambanis (2000), note 69 above.

92   de Waal, note 10 above.

93   It is essential to acknowledge that in poor countries external actors are active stakeholders in the domestic policy arena through agenda setting and orchestrating alliances between interested players. Lise Rakner, "Methods for analyzing power", in Division for Democratic Governance, *Methods for Analyzing Power – A Workshop Report*, SIDA, Stockholm, May 2005, p. 18.

94   Doyle and Sambanis (2000), note 69 above; Doyle and Sambanis (2006), note 69 above.

95   Berdal, note 63 above; Spear, note 6 above.

96   Britain resumed its role as Sierra Leone's largest bilateral donor in the immediate post-conflict period, and was viewed as an "aid darling" among UN member states. DFID (the UK Department for International Development) channelled an average of about £50 million (US$79.53 million) of aid per year to Sierra Leone from 2000 until 2010. Jimmy Kandeh, "Intervention and peacebuilding in Sierra Leone: A critical perspective", in Tunde Zack-Williams (ed.), *When the State Fails: Studies on Intervention in the Sierra Leone Civil War* (Chicago, IL: University of Chicago Press, 2012), p. 98. As much as 39 per cent of DFID funding went directly to budget support to the Sierra Leonean government.

97   Weinstein, note 70 above.

98   Walter, note 70 above; Walter, note 80 above.

99   As Fortna states, "factions often make decisions with incomplete information in the face of uncertainty about their opponents, about the likely actions of peacekeepers, or about the outcomes of future political processes". Fortna, note 60 above, p. 81.

100 Doyle and Sambanis (2000), note 69 above; Berdal, note 63 above.

101 Doyle and Sambanis, ibid., p. 787; Doyle and Sambanis (2006), note 69 above.

102 On the process-tracing methodology see Alexander L. George and Andrew Bennett, *Case Studies and Theory Development in the Social Sciences* (Cambridge, MA: MIT Press, 2005). As Tansey points out, the process-tracing method can highlight where political developments were generated primarily by domestic or international actors, or a combination of both. Oisin Tansey, "Evaluating the legacies of state-building: Success, failure, and the role of responsibility", *International Studies Quarterly*, Vol. 58, No. 1 (2014), pp. 174–186.

103 See Paul Richards, *Fighting for the Rainforest* (Oxford: International African Institute in association with James Currey, 1996); Zubairu Wai, *Epistemologies of African Conflicts: Violence, Evolutionism, and the War in Sierra Leone* (London: Palgrave, 2012), pp. 94–112; David Keen, *Conflict and Collusion* (Oxford: James Currey, 2005); Lansana Gberie, *A Dirty War in West Africa: The RUF and the Destruction of Sierra Leone* (Bloomington, IN: Indiana University Press, 2005).

104 See Ibrahim Abdullah and Ismail Rashid, "Smallest victims, youngest killers: Juvenile combatants in Sierra Leone's civil war", in Ibrahim Abdullah (ed.), *Between Democracy and Terror: The Sierra Leone Civil War* (Dakar: Codesria Books, 2004), pp. 238–253; John Hirsch, *Sierra Leone: Diamonds and the Struggle for Democracy* (Boulder, CO: Lynne Rienner, 2001); Keen, ibid.; Gberie, ibid.; John-Peter Pham, *Child Soldiers, Adult Interests: The Global Dimensions of the Sierra Leonean Tragedy* (New York: Nova Science Publishers, 2005).

105 This alliance was comprised of members of the AFRC, which overthrew the Kabbah state in May 1997, and the rebel RUF.

106 Lomé peace accords, cited in Hirsch, note 104 above, p. 135–157.

107 Paul Richards and James Vincent, "Sierra Leone: Marginalization of the RUF", in Jeroen de Zeeuw (ed.), *From Soldiers to Politicians: Transforming Rebel Movements After War* (Boulder, CO: Lynne Rienner, 2008), p. 88.

108 'Funmi Olonisakin, *Peacekeeping in Sierra Leone: The Story of UNAMSIL* (Boulder, CO: Lynne Rienner, 2008); Wai, note 103 above, p. 111.

109 Lansana Gberie, "Destabilizing Guinea", Partnership Africa Canada Occasional Paper No. 1, 2001, www.pacweb.org/Documents/diamonds_KP/1_dastabilizing_Guinea_Eng_Oct2001.pdf.

110 Wai, note 103 above, p. 112.

111 Andrew M. Dorman, *Blair's Successful War: British Military Intervention in Sierra Leone* (Farnham: Ashgate Publishing, 2009); William Fowler, *Certain Death in Sierra Leone: The SAS and Operation Barass 2000* (Oxford: Osprey Publishing, 2010).

112 Underlying the Kabbah state was a robust political settlement with demonstrated commitment and support for President Kabbah. This settlement, which dated back before the 1996 elections, involved prominent members of the SLPP. The party's mechanisms also helped the state to overcome collective action problems.

113 The poor state of the Sierra Leonean economy severely constrained the immediate transition period. The protracted 11-year conflict took a devastating toll on all facets of life, from social and economic development to infrastructure and human capacity. See UN data on Sierra Leone, http://data.un.org/CountryProfile.aspx?crName=SIERRA%20LEONE.

114 The British government was deeply invested in Kabbah's presidency. As far back as 1996, President Kabbah requested assistance from the UK to support his central government's weak capacity to enforce domestic order in the country. When Kabbah was exiled in Conakry for nine months, the UK and the United States bankrolled his government. British and US support through the United Nations was essential to tilting the balance of power in favour of the Kabbah state.

115 UNAMSIL was one of the largest UN peacekeeping missions in the world at the time. The UN spent US$2.775 billion on its operations from 1998 until the end of December 2005. United Nations, "Assessment of Member States' contributions for the financing of the United Nations Observer Mission in Sierra Leone (UNOMSIL) and the United Nations Mission in Sierra Leone (UNAMSIL)", New York, 30 November 2004, UN Doc. ST/ADM/

SER.B/537. After the war the government of Sierra Leone's budget was initially almost entirely dependent on foreign aid (2000–2001).

116 General elections in Sierra Leone are organized every five years. With Kabbah's mandate coming to a close around March 2001 and Britain's unwillingness to establish a formal trusteeship over Sierra Leone, preparations for multiparty elections appeared to be the most viable option to forge a political settlement that reflected local realities.

117 A national electoral commission was established, albeit with substantial financial support from international donors.

118 Institutions associated with DDR were in place in early 2001. However, the focus of this section is on the third phase of DDR when the disarmament was accelerated.

119 The lack of strong political and military leadership within the RUF meant that international and regional actors agreed to recognize Issa Sesay as interim leader of the RUF in mid-2000 and pursued a "political buy-in" strategy with him, Kallon and Gbao. Author's confidential interview with former NCDDR official, 23 December 2011.

120 Special material incentives (now known as "commander incentive packages" in UN language) were used by the NCDDR to ensure the RUF's buy-in, according to the government, to "satisfy the ambitions of the fighting forces, which are undefined and/or greater than what was negotiated". "NCDDR policy issues for NCDDR consideration", 23 August 2000, p. 2, National Archives of Sierra Leone, Freetown, archive document 642 in author's possession.

121 Policy development was left to the government and appropriate international bodies, including staff from UNDP and the World Bank.

122 The reintegration phase was funded through the Multi-Donor Trust Fund established and managed by the World Bank. The majority of funds for Sierra Leone's DDR process was procured from external donors, which meant that external actors had significant control over the DDR programme.

123 Gebreselassie Tesfamichael, Nicole Ball and Julie Nenon, "Peace in Sierra Leone: Evaluating the disarmament, development, and reintegration process, final evaluation of Disarmament, Demobilization and Reintegration Program and the Multi-Donor Trust Fund supporting DDR", Creative Associates, Washington, DC, October 2004, p. 70. The World Bank retained majority control over the Multi-Donor Trust Fund and decisions related to how funds were distributed. See also NCDDR archives, National Archives of Sierra Leone, Freetown, archive document 625 in author's possession.

124 NCDDR document on the post-May 2001 DDR, p. 3, National Archives of Sierra Leone, Freetown, archive document 625 in author's possession.

125 The government of Sierra Leone wrote regular position papers in advance of each Tripartite meeting, commenting on the need continually to test the RUF's level of commitment towards the peace process. At the start of each Tripartite meeting it became customary for the government to provide a briefing on its own perception of the security situation in the country.

126 For instance, in July 2001, when momentum for disarmament was gathering, the government released 33 RUF detainees from prison. The RUF's level of commitment could be partially measured by its increased representation and participation at the Tripartite talks from July 2001 onwards. At the July 2001 meeting in Bo, a schedule for disarmament was drafted based on input from the RUF and CDF and a timetable was established in which two districts (one RUF and one CDF stronghold) would be disarmed at the same time within a period of 31 days. See Executive Secretary NDCCR notes from 17 July 2001

Joint Commission meeting on DDR, National Archives of Sierra Leone, Freetown, archive document 927 in author's possession.

127 Early in the disarmament and demobilization phase, three "liaison officers" (one from each faction) were incorporated into the NCDDR Executive Secretariat and paid monthly salaries. NCDDR archival notes in author's possession, 18 November 2011.

128 Author's confidential interviews with former NCDDR official, Freetown, February 2012; Tesfamichael et al., note 124 above. A review of NCDDR archives reveals that Issa Sesay nominated six members of the RUF to serve as staff members in the NCDDR on 15 June 2001. These RUF members were integrated into the NCDDR on 19 June. Their role was to verify the identity of demobilized combatants who had been previously screened by the faction's high command for subsequent reintegration assistance. Equal numbers of CDF were integrated in the north and at headquarters.

129 There were mixed perceptions about whether this was an effective strategy or not. Independent consultants claim that their integration in the governance system was "limited". Testfamichael et al., ibid.

130 Report of the Executive Secretary NCDDR to the Joint Commission on DDR, 17 July 2001, p. 9, National Archives of Sierra Leone, Freetown, archive document 909 in author's possession.

131 Its composition also included UNICEF, the National Commission for Rehabilitation, Reconstruction and Reintegration, UNAMSIL, the European Union, DFID, UNDP, the UN High Commissioner for Refugees and various international and local NGOs.

132 One of the issues that the TCCs dealt with was destruction of weapons collected. Since UNAMSIL did not have the technical expertise to perform this task, DFID provided a weapons disposal expert to advise on the handling of weapons and ammunition collected since 20 October 1999. NCDDR, "Policy issues for DDR", 30 April 1999, National Archives of Sierra Leone, Freetown, in author's possession.

133 The TCCs received orders from the Tripartite on issues and filtered information upwards when logistical constraints affected the scheduling and logistics of implementing disarmament. Report of the Executive Secretary NCDDR, 18 September 2001, p. 4, National Archives of Sierra Leone, Freetown, archive document 836 in author's possession.

134 Wai, note 103 above.

135 Ministry of Internal Affairs/Sierra Leone Police, "Community Arms Collection and Destruction Programme (CACD) concept paper", October 2001, p. 1, National Archives of Sierra Leone, Freetown, in author's possession.

136 Alhaji M. S. Bah, "Micro-disarmament in West Africa: The ECOWAS moratorium on small arms and light weapons", *African Security Review*, Vol. 13, No. 3 (2004), p. 16.

137 Derek Miller, Daniel Ladoucer and Zoe Dugal, "From research to road map: Learning from the arms for development initiative in Sierra Leone", UNIDIR/UNDP, Geneva, 2003, pp. 14, 16; Mark Malan, Sarah Meek, Thokozani Thusi, Jeremy Ginifer and Patrick Coker, "Sierra Leone: Building the road to recovery", Institute for Security Studies Monograph 80, Pretoria, 2003, p. 29.

138 Ministry of Internal Affairs/Sierra Leone Police, note 136 above.

139 Bah, note 137 above, p. 40.

140 Ibid.

141 A third arms reduction programme was implemented in November 2002, driven by the UNDP office in Sierra Leone. From 2003 to 2008 UNDP assisted the Ministry of Internal

Affairs legal department to develop legislation for regulations on arms, ammunitions and explosives and modernize the Sierra Leonean national armament legislation (the Arms and Ammunition Ordinance 1955 No. 14 and the Explosive Ordinance 1955 No. 15). The process was stalled for unclear political reasons. Bah, note 137 above, p. 45, fn 29; author's confidential interviews with National Commission for Small Arms officials, Freetown, November–December 2011. The single-barrel shotguns remained in the custody of the police until the executive and parliament approved the new licensing system in 2013.

142 Ministry of Internal Affairs/Sierra Leone Police, note 136 above.

143 Bah, note 137 above, p. 41.

144 Ministry of Internal Affairs/Sierra Leone Police, note 136 above, p. 2. The NCDDR provided logistical and technical support to the SLP to enable the collection of arms and ammunition from individuals who did not qualify for the DDR programme.

145 Kabbah's mandate from the 1996 elections had been disrupted by the May 1997 coup and extended several times already, as agreed by the UN. On the elections see David Harris, *Sierra Leone: A Political History* (London: Hurst, 2013), pp. 119–125.

146 Key international donors insisted on the need for elections, despite being only six months removed from war. Local civil society groups in Sierra Leone voiced their opposition to the timetable and proposed delaying the elections until reconciliation was under way, but this proposal fell on deaf ears.

147 The 2002 elections left no questions about the irrelevancy and disintegration of the RUF as a political movement. The RUF Party (now an official political party) received 1.7 per cent of the popular vote in the 14 May 2002 presidential elections and 2.2 per cent of the vote in the parliamentary elections held at the same time.

148 In the May 2002 presidential elections the majority of soldiers and police officers voted for Kabbah's opponents. To a large extent, reforms undertaken by the British insulated Kabbah from establishing a political settlement with the army to guarantee its loyal and unity.

149 von Dyck, note 111 above.

150 As one report noted, "Without the support of the UN peace mission and donors, the government would almost certainly collapse; owing to their presence, it will survive." Economist Intelligence Unit, "Country report Sierra Leone", September 2003, p. 2.

151 von Dyck, note 111 above.

152 Ibid.

153 Ibid.

154 The December 1999 pay schedule included 3,340 soldiers. Sierra Leone Security Sector Programme, "A paper on handling the ex-SLA", 8 January 2000, p. 1, National Archives of Sierra Leone, Freetown, in author's possession.

155 Minutes of a meeting on military reintegration, 20 January 2000, MOD archives, in author's possession.

156 After this deadline, any soldiers or officers who failed to report to work were to be considered discharged. Confidential government document on the peace process, 14 May 2001, p. 1, National Archives of Sierra Leone, Freetown, archive document 630 in author's possession.

157 Peter Albrecht and Paul Jackson, "Security system transformation in Sierra Leone, 1997–2007", Global Facilitation Network for Security Sector Reform, University of Birmingham, Birmingham, February 2009; Osman Gbla, "Security sector reform under international tutelage in Sierra Leone", *International Peacekeeping*, Vol. 13, No. 1 (2006), p. 78.

158 Unlike in the past, civilians occupied senior positions in the military's bureaucracy. IMATT set up a civilian structure within the MOD modelled after the UK MOD. The director-general is the government's principal adviser on defence matters with primary responsibility for policy, finance, procurement and administration. He/she also serves as the principal accounting officer responsible to the minister of defence for the overall organization, management and staffing of the department. This officer is responsible for reporting to parliament on expenditures related to the military. Gbla, ibid., p. 84.

159 Malan et al., note 138 above.

160 IMATT recommended against any major demobilization of the RSLAF during this period to prevent destabilization of the security environment.

161 The inspector-general of the SLP was British ex-police officer Keith Biddle from 1999 to 2003. The bulk of the SLP reforms took place in 2000–2005, during which period the UK spent approximately £25 million on the police alone. Albrecht and Jackson, note 158 above; Peter Albrecht, "Transforming internal security in Sierra Leone: Sierra Leone Police and broader justice sector reform", Danish Institute for International Studies, Copenhagen, 2010, p. 12. Biddle insisted on direct access to President Kabbah as a condition for his support for the reform process.

162 The civilian reintegration was not well planned or executed. It suffered from too short a training period, and the quality of training offered was inadequate. See Tesfamichael et al., note 124 above; Simon Arthy, "DFID funded reintegration activities in Sierra Leone: Reintegration lesson learning impact evaluation", DFID, London, 2003.

163 Kabbah appointed Hinga Norman as deputy defence minister in May 1997. Norman had used his influence to shape early recruitment decisions in the RSLAF military reform efforts in 1999.

164 von Dyck, note 111 above.

165 Report of a meeting on the status of the ex-SLA held at the presidential lodge, 16 December 1999, p. 1, National Archives of Sierra Leone, Freetown, archive document 737 in author's possession.

166 MOD archive document in author's possession.

167 See SILSEP, "Development of a basing strategy for the restructured Republic of Sierra Leone Armed Forces (RSLAF)", sent to deputy minister of defence, chief of defence staff and national security adviser, 1 January 2000, National Archives of Sierra Leone, Freetown, archive document 730 in author's possession.

168 One of the top priorities for the UK was to discern strategies for basing requirements for the RSLAF. A team of UK military works advisers was sent to Freetown in January–February 2000 to assess options and make recommendations on the location/basing of RSLAF units by 14 February 2000.

169 However, former RUF and CDF could join the SLP later on provided they successfully passed the same entry requirements established for all cadets. Jonathan Friedman, "Building strategic capacity in the police: Sierra Leone, 1998–2008", Princeton University Innovations for Successful Societies, 2008, www.princeton.edu/successfulsocieties/content/focusareas/PL/policynotes/view.xml?id=181, p. 5.

170 Albrecht and Jackson, note 158 above.

171 During the political negotiations, some guidelines for handling the military reform were discussed. International and regional mediators encouraged discussion on a quota system for the warring factions, but the proposals were rejected because the parties could not come to an agreement.

172 Lomé peace accord, Article 16. See Hirsch, note 104 above, appendix.

173 Lomé peace accord, ibid., Article 17.

174 Government of Sierra Leone, "Policy clarification on combatant participation in the DDR program *vis-à-vis* the restructured army", no date, p. 1, NCDDR/MOD archives, National Archives of Sierra Leone, Freetown, archive document 712 in author's possession.

175 Ibid., p. 2.

176 Ibid.

177 British officer Colonel P. R. Farrar stepped into the role of assistant chief of staff (training) in Sierra Leone's MOD. He was responsible for implementing the MRP on behalf of IMATT.

178 SLAF training directive for MRPG 2, 16 December 2001, MOD/SLAF archives, National Archives of Sierra Leone, Freetown, archive document MRP 035 in author's possession.

179 Ibid.

180 Roughly two-thirds (67 per cent) of these recruits came from the RUF, while the rest were ex-CDF. Albrecht and Jackson, note 158 above, p. 66, table 2. The overall ratio of RUF/CDF was 65:35.

181 MRP soldiers were given ranks no higher than corporal regardless of previous experience and training before or during the war. This was to avoid creating resentment among the rank and file and the newly trained soldiers. Author's confidential interview with a senior defence official involved in the process, Freetown, 2 December 2011.

182 MOD archives in author's possession

183 NCDDR/MOD archives, National Archives of Sierra Leone, Freetown, archive document 712 in author's possession.

184 Ibid.

185 Letter from Francis Kai-Kai to Colonel Tom Carew, 5 December 2000, NCDDR archives, National Archives of Sierra Leone, Freetown, archive document MRP 005 in author's possession.

186 NCDDR/MOD archives, National Archives of Sierra Leone, Freetown, archive document 712 in author's possession.

187 Ibid.

188 Keen, note 103 above, p. 284; Albrecht and Jackson, note 158 above, p. 66.

189 International Crisis Group, "Managing uncertainty", Africa Report No. 35, Freetown/Brussels, 24 October 2001, p. 12.

190 Michael Mann defines infrastructural power in terms of a central government's "institutional capacity ... to penetrate its territories and logistically implement decisions". Michael Mann, "The autonomous power of the state: Its origins, mechanisms and results", *Archives européennes de sociologie*, Vol. 25 (1984), pp. 185–213.

191 It is beyond the scope of this paper to review the entire SSR process in Sierra Leone. For reviews of some core components see Albrecht and Jackson, note 158 above; Gbla, note 158 above. For a critical review of the relationship between statebuilding and SSR in Sierra Leone see von Dyck, note 111 above.

192 Taylor's faction was weakened militarily and could only hold on to some territory in central Monrovia. The anti-Taylor LURD force controlled over 60 per cent of the country and launched attacks on Monrovia in April 2003. The military ceasefire was agreed on 17 June 2003. All three factions, including Taylor's former regime, represented a narrow section of Liberians.

193 Author's personal interview with former Liberian government official, Monrovia, 13 March 2012.

194 The International Contact Group was led by the United States and Nigeria and comprised ECOWAS, the UN, the African Union, the European Union, France, the UK, Ghana, Morocco and Senegal.

195 The AFL, LNP, National Security Agency, National Bureau of Investigation, Special Security Service, Drugs Enforcement Agency, National Fire Service, Ministry of National Security, Bureau of Immigration and Naturalization, Bureau of Customs and Excise and Monrovia City Police. Judy Smith-Hölm, *Rebuilding the Security Sector in Post-Conflict Societies* (Munster: LIT Verlag, 2010), pp. 76–77.

196 Liberia's GNI per capita grew from $250 to $271, $316 and $341 from 2005 to 2008. It was just over $1/day in 2009, and rose to $452 in 2011 and $480 in 2012 (based on World Bank and UN data, http://data.un.org/CountryProfile.aspx?crName=liberia).

197 At the political negotiations, each faction was represented by a 10-person delegation. Charles Taylor took part in the early rounds of negotiations until the UN-backed Special Court for Sierra Leone announced an indictment against him in the middle of the talks. Taylor immediately left the talks and flew back to Monrovia. Desirée Nilsson, "Crafting a secure peace – Evaluating Liberia's Comprehensive Peace Agreement 2003", Department of Peace and Conflict Research, Uppsala University, Uppsala, 2009, p. 23. On 10 August 2003 Taylor announced from his executive mansion in Monrovia that he would step down and accept asylum in Nigeria on an invitation from Nigerian President Olusegun Obsanajo. Taylor handed over power to Vice President Moses Blah on 11 August 2003. Author's personal interview with a high-ranking government of Liberia delegate, 15 March 2012.

198 LURD's 10-person delegation was headed by Kabineh Janneh (appointed as minister of justice and subsequently appointed to the supreme court in 2006).

199 Leaders of the Krahn tribe split from LURD in 2002–2003 to form their own movement to pursue power as an independent movement. MODEL's 10-person delegation was headed by Thomas Yaya Nimely (later appointed as minister of foreign affairs).

200 Stephen Ellis, *The Mask of Anarchy: The Destruction of Liberia and the Religious Dimension of an African Civil War* (London: Hurst & Co., 1999).

201 Civil society and religious groups included the Mano River Women Peace Network, the Liberian Bar Association and the Inter-religious Council for Liberians. Nilsson, note 198 above, p. 22.

202 Twenty-one ministerial positions and the 42 deputy and assistant ministerial positions were divided up among the Liberian stakeholders. LURD received the speaker of the House in the legislation, while Taylor's former minister of justice (Eddington Varmah) became deputy speaker.

203 Thomas Jaye, "An analysis of post-Taylor politics", *Review of African Political Economy*, Vol. 30, No. 98 (2003), p. 644.

204 "Peace agreement between the Government of Liberia, the Liberians United for Reconciliation and Democracy, the Movement for Democracy in Liberia and the political parties", Accra, 18 August 2003, UN Doc. S/2003/850, Article XXIV.

205 According to the rules, one faction was given a ministerial head position, while the two deputy positions (for administration and operations) were given to the two other factions.

206 Morten Bøas, "Making plans for Liberia – A trusteeship approach to good governance?", *Third World Quarterly*, Vol. 30, No. 7 (2009), pp. 1329–1341.

207 It was obvious to the International Contact Group at the time that transitional government officials were misappropriating funds for their own benefit. A few years later a team from ECOWAS investigated financial practices during the transitional period and implicated

NTGL officials. United Nations, "Fourteenth progress report of the UN Secretary-General on the United Nations Mission in Liberia", 15 March 2007, UN Doc. S/2007/151, p. 2.

208 According to a senior Liberian government official, the balance of forces in Monrovia at the time were dispersed among three main zones based on informal arrangements and territorial control. The factions set up liaison offices in their rivals' territory to facilitate consultation meetings between the forces. Author's confidential interviews with former faction commanders, Monrovia, 17 April 2012.

209 At the time the DDR implementation framework was designed, the UN authorities viewed most national institutions as "paralysed" as a result of the conflict.

210 Christian Bugnion, Luc Lafrenière, Sam Gbaydee, Hirut Tefferi and Cerue Garlo, "External mid-term evaluation report of the Disarmament, Demobilization, Rehabilitation and Reintegration Programme in Liberia", UNDP, New York, 2 October 2006, pp. 9, 23.

211 The conditions after the war were such that most of Taylor's combatants were based in Monrovia. LURD was based mostly in the northwest (Lofa county) and MODEL combatants were in the southeast (Sinoe and Zwedru).

212 The UN's policy is to provide $150 immediately upon disarmament and the additional $150 after completing the reintegration component. This information was not communicated clearly to the combatants.

213 Kathleen Jennings, "The struggle to satisfy: DDR through the eyes of ex-combatants in Liberia", *International Peacekeeping*, Vol. 14, No. 2 (2007), pp. 204–218 at p. 208; author's personal interview with former NTGL official, Monrovia, 13 March 2012.

214 Order was restored quite efficiently because the command structure of the former government of Liberia was arguably best suited to solve collective action problems. The leaders (Daniel Chea and Moses Blah) instructed Roland Duo and Coco Denis to mobilize a special taskforce of 30–40 men to disarm the combatants forcefully. Some combatants were disarmed in this way, while others were bribed with cash to give up their arms. Author's personal interview with former NTGL official, Monrovia, 17 April 2012. The UN paid US$75 in crisp new US bills that had been flown specifically to Monrovia in exchange for each weapon collected as the first instalment of a total demobilization allowance of $300. Author's personal interview with DAC official, Monrovia, 13 March 2013.

215 US plans for Liberia's transition started being drawn up in late 2003 when the Department of Defense and the State Department created an interagency working group on Liberia.

216 The most important donors to the International Contact Group on Liberia were the International Monetary Fund, the World Bank, the European Union and the United States.

217 For a similar argument and more comprehensive application of this idea to Somalia see Aisha Ahmad, "Agenda for peace or budget for war? Evaluating the economic impact of international intervention in Somalia", *International Journal*, Vol. 67, No. 2 (2012), p. 313.

218 Philip Bartholomew, "Reconstructing central banking in war-torn Liberia", in Charles Enoch, Karl Friedrich Habermeier and Marta de Castello Branco (eds), *Building Monetary and Financial Systems: Case Studies in Technical Assistance* (Washington, DC: IMF, 2007), p. 68.

219 The transitional government's contribution was approximately US$2.173 million. Cited in the NTGL contribution to the DDRR programme: April 2004–October 2005, NCDDRR archives, National Archives of Sierra Leone, Freetown, archive document 0157 in author's possession.

220 According to one key official involved in the Liberian DDRR programme, the UN used a "cut-and-paste" model in Liberia. Interview with former special assistant to the former executive director of the NCDDRR, Monrovia, 17 February 2012.

221 The three warring factions agreed in Accra during political negotiations to appoint Jarbo as executive director of the NCDDRR. Author's personal interview with former NCDDRR official, Monrovia, February 2012.

222 The NCDDRR policy committee met to discuss specific concerns of the parties, endorsed specific policy issues and adopted the joint operation plan.

223 NCDDRR archives in author's possession.

224 The JIU structure consisted of four units: disarmament and demobilization (UNMIL lead), staffed by military peacekeepers, observers and experts; rehabilitation and reintegration (JIU/UNDP lead), staffed mostly by UNDP reintegration experts; monitoring and evaluation (JIU/UNDP lead); and information and sensitization (JIU/OCHA lead), staffed by the Office for the Coordination of Humanitarian Affairs.

225 Author's confidential interviews with NCDDR officials, Monrovia, March 2012.

226 NCDDRR archives in author's possession.

227 Jarbo suggested that the UN should rely on the junior commanders in the field to implement DDR, according to three high-level NCDDRR officials from the "48 Generals" interviewed by the author who were deeply involved in the process.

228 Author's confidential interviews with former high-level NCDDRR official, Monrovia, March 2012; confirmed by Nicole Ball and Dylan Hendrickson, "Review of international financing arrangements for disarmament, demobilization and reintegration", Phase 2 report to Working Group 2, Stockholm Initiative on Disarmament, Demobilization and Reintegration, Stockholm, 26 September 2005, p. 34. UNDP maintained control over NCDDR funds by channelling money through a UNDP trust fund as opposed to allowing it to go through NTGL coffers.

229 NCDDRR archives in author's possession

230 On 29 October 2003 UNMIL's budget was prepared and approved by the UN Security Council. The budget allocated provisions for a phased deployment of 14,785 military personnel, 215 military observers, 1,115 civilian police and 893 international civilian personnel (including 286 UN volunteers), and hired 768 national staff. UNMIL became one of the most expensive peacekeeping operations in the world, with an annual budget of about US$700 million.

231 Nichols estimates that approximately 64 per cent of the weapons shipped to Liberia during the war were collected during DDR. Ryan Nichols, "Disarming Liberia: Progress and pitfalls", in *Armed and Aimless* (Geneva: Small Arms Survey, 2005), p. 124. According to the 2004 UN Panel of Experts, about 60 per cent of the weapons in Liberia were collected. UN Panel of Experts, "Report on Liberia", 6 December 2004, UN Doc. S/2004/955.

232 Nichols, ibid.; Jennings, note 215 above.

233 There were numerous inconsistencies applied during the disarmament process by UNMIL MILOBS, resulting in large numbers of non-combatants benefiting from the DDR programme. Additionally. UNMIL was hampered by significant logistical constraints, which contributed to a low weapon-to-combatant ratio.

234 In local parlance, Sierra Leoneans call these organizations "suitcase NGOs" to signify the fact that one person, who is the head of the organization, carries with him/her a briefcase containing all the important paperwork related to finances, etc., such that no one else has access. On the briefcase NGO business model see Ahmad, note 219 above, pp. 325–326.

235 Alexander Loden, "Civil society and security sector reform in post-conflict Liberia: Painting a moving train without brushes", *International Journal of Transitional Justice*, Vol. 1 (2007), p. 304.

236 Arthy, note 163 above.

237 Author's interviews with various former combatants in Freetown, Kono and Bo, November 2011–February 2012.

238 National Defense Research Institute, "Making Liberia safe: Transformation of the national security sector", RAND/National Defence Research Institute, 2007, www.rand.org/content/dam/rand/pubs/monographs/2007/RAND_MG529.pdf.

239 Mark Malan, "Security sector reform in Liberia: Mixed results from humble beginnings", Strategic Studies Institute, US Army War College, Carlisle, PA, 2008.

240 Major tasks have included responding to calls, investigating crimes and attending crime scenes, demonstrating respect for human rights, administering police records and doing community policing. UN Special Representative to the Secretary-General, "Report on Liberia", 22 March 2004, UN Doc. S/2004/229, p. 7.

241 An American police chief, Mark Kroeker from Los Angeles, served as UN CivPol's commander. UN CivPol began its mission in December 2003, and 20 former Liberian police officers who had been selected and screened by UN CivPol were retained and received training from UN trainers for three days to conduct joint patrols with UNMIL. IRIN, "Liberia: UNMIL retrains first batch of Liberian police", IRIN, 3 December 2003.

242 Author's confidential interviews with Liberian security officials, Monrovia, March 2012.

243 IRIN, "Liberia: UN provides crash training for 400 police officers", IRIN, 12 January 2004; Malan, note 241 above, p. 48.

244 United Nations, "Second progress report of the Secretary-General on the United Nations Mission in Liberia", 22 March 2004.

245 Since UNMIL funding was directed to other priorities, the severance packages for former "state" security personnel were sourced from range of donor countries, notably the US and South African governments.

246 UNMIL progress reports, 2003–2007, www.un.org/en/peacekeeping/missions/unmil/reports.shtml.

247 The eligibility criteria included proof of Liberian citizenship, proof of age between 18 and 35 years and proof of high-school graduation. Recruits had to be "mentally and physically fit", and all candidates had to relinquish any formal positions held in a political party.

248 Malan, note 241 above, pp. 50–51.

249 Sean McFate, "Outsourcing the mking of militaries: DynCorp International as sovereign agent", *Review of African Political Economy*, Vol. 35, No. 118 (2008), p. 645; Malan, note 241 above, p. 32.

250 Alix Julia Boucher, "Defence sector reform: A note on current practice", 12 December 2009, Henry L. Stimson Center, Washington, DC, p. 4.

251 See Adedeji Ebo, "Local ownership and emerging trends in SSR: A case study of outsourcing in Liberia", in Donais, note 10 above, pp. 161–162.

252 The CPA made clear that international and regional actors would play a crucial role in providing advice and support throughout the reform process. The leaders of the three factions agreed to hand over responsibility to the US to lead the AFL reform process. See Peace Agreement, note 205 above, Article VII, Section 1(b).

253 The AFL is structured similarly to the US Army.

254 Author's interview with former DAC official, Monrovia, 13 March 2013; McFate, note 251 above, p. 648.

255 United Nations, "Third progress report of the Secretary-General on the United Nations Mission in Liberia", 26 May 2004, UN Doc. S/2004/430, p. 8.

256 The minister of defence was allocated to the former government of Liberia (Daniel Chea), while LURD's representative (Joe Wylie) became deputy minister for administration. MODEL's Brown Parjebo became deputy defence of operations. LURD's leadership insisted that their chief of staff, Aliyu Mohammed Sheriff (Cobra), be appointed as chief of staff of the AFL during the transitional period (a largely ceremonial position). In October 2003 LURD cut off NGO and UNMIL movement to Tubmanburg and threatened to renew the conflict. International Crisis Group, "Liberia: Security challenges", *ICG Africa Report*, Issue 71 (2003), p. 10. Within one month of the establishment of the NTGL there was infighting between Sheriff (LURD) and Konneh (MODEL) over who should be the AFL chief of staff. However, the accord made no specific provision for the allocation of government jobs immediately below these levels. This later became a contentious issue in late November 2003 when leaders of the factions refused to disarm their forces until assistant minister posts were allocated equitably among the three factions. IRIN, "US envoy asked to intervene in disarmament dispute", IRIN, 28 November 2003.

257 The Liberian Defence Advisory Committee comprised the chiefs of staff of the former government forces, LURD and MODEL as part of the NTGL that served under the authority of the MOD. The DAC was tasked to develop proposals for the reform of Liberia's armed forces to address issues of demobilization and restructuring. United Nations, "First progress report of the Secretary-General on the United Nations Mission in Liberia", 15 December 2003, UN Doc. S/2003/1175, p. 15.

258 Author's personal interview with former DAC official, Monrovia, 13 March 2012.

259 PAE had been awarded a contract to provide ECOMOG with logistical support in Sierra Leone since mid-1998. PAE was responsible for supporting the AFL, training the officers and non-commissioned officers and providing mentorship to the new AFL. Both agencies were mandated to lead in reconstruction of military barracks and other military facilities.

260 DynCorp was responsible for assisting in the demobilization of the old AFL as well as recruitment, vetting and training of new AFL soldiers and new Ministry of National Defence civilian recruits.

261 Twenty-one out of 23 staff on the team were retired US Army personnel. According to an American insider involved in the process, "the majority of officers who served on the assessment mission had never set foot in Africa before". McFate, note 251 above, p. 646.

262 Ibid., p. 652.

263 As Ebo points out, DynCorp's role in Liberia marked the first time in the history of West Africa that a private military company had been contracted to restructure and train a national army. Ebo, note 253 above, p. 37.

264 In the MOD Taylor's defence minister, Daniel Chea, retained his position, as did the former chief of staff, Kpenkpah Y. Konah. The LURD faction was represented by Joe Wylie (as deputy minister for administration), and the MODEL faction by Brown Parjebo (deputy minister of operations). These officials jockeyed for political relevance within the ministry. Due to the nature of the precarious power-sharing arrangement within the NTGL, power struggles between LURD, MODEL and former government of Liberia factional leaders kept the MOD and DAC from executing effective strategies and policies for reforming the AFL.

265 Ryan Welken, "Rebuilding the Armed Forces of Liberia: An assessment of the Liberia Security Sector Reform Program", Naval Postgraduate School, California, 2010, p. 23. The Leahy Amendment requires that all foreign troops trained by US military be pre-screened by the US State Department for human rights violations allegations. Moreover, the Leahy Amendment requires that the instruction US military troops provide includes training in

human rights and laws of land warfare. US military troops are also required to report any evidence of human rights violations.

266 Author's confidential interview with former DAC official, Monrovia, 13 March 2012.

267 These officers allegedly included their family members and friends on the list. Author's confidential interview with former DAC officials, Monrovia, March 2012.

268 The first criterion applied was age. Since there is no Liberian military law, the US military mandatory retirement at age 65 was applied to the demobilization phase. The second criterion, based on seniority, identified all soldiers who had served for an accumulated time of 25 years. The third criterion applied was education qualifications: DAC officials set a minimum education requirement of high-school graduation. Author's interview with former DAC official, Monrovia, 13 March 2012. There was a discrepancy in the number of Liberian soldiers. According to the Liberian redocumentation exercise, there were a total of 14,684 soldiers in the AFL. Author's confidential interviews, Monrovia, March 2012. According to DynCorp, however, the AFL strength was closer to 13,770 soldiers. See McFate, note 251 above.

269 Chairman Bryant explained "Following the April 12, 1980 *coup d'état*, the merit system in the AFL was compromised and there was a distortion in the table of organization and equipment of the army." Africa News Service, "Dissolve or not to dissolve, AFL gives the dying horse's kick", *The Analyst*, 4 January 2006.

270 Joe Wylie, deputy defence minister for administration in the NTGL, explained, "You cannot dissolve the army. I kept telling Bryant 'don't dissolve'. And if we have a small retained strength of 1,000 men, that will resolve the problem. Nobody listened to us." Joe Wylie, truth and reconciliation testimony, Monsterrado County, 22 August 2008, http://trcofliberia.org/videos/1348.

271 Boucher, note 252 above, p. 17.

272 Thomas Dempsey, "Security sector reform in Liberia", Ocnus – Defence & Arms, 16 December 2006, www.ocnus.net/artman2/publish/Defence_Arms_13/Security_Sector_Reform_in_Liberia_27136_printer.shtml.

273 Local ownership of the SSR programme in Liberia was not taken into consideration by US authorities. The interim deputy minister of defence (administration) spoke about the lack of transparency of the MOU between the NTGL and the US government in 2004: "They didn't even allow me to see it [the MOU] as deputy minister of administration. I raised an issue with that. And, the DynCorp guys said they were only answerable to the US government. The USG is answerable to the Liberian government not to the ministerial staff." Author's confidential interview, Monrovia, 12 March 2012.

274 Thomas Jaye, "An assessment report on security sector reform in Liberia", Governance Reform Commission of Liberia, Monrovia, 23 September 2006; Adedeji Ebo, *The Challenges and Opportunities of Security Sector Reform in Post-Conflict Liberia* (Geneva: DCAF, 2005), p. 19.

275 United Nations, "Ninth progress report of the Secretary-General on the United Nations Mission in Liberia", 7 December 2005, UN Doc. S/2005/764. As a consequence of the delays their jobs did not start until 2007.

276 For instance, Ellen Johnson-Sirleaf initially requested the Governance Reform Commission (GRC) to conduct comprehensive national consultations towards developing a national security strategy and architecture in 2006–2007. The GRC held a series of consultations with security agencies, government bodies, international partners and civil society stakeholders on 3–4 April 2006 involving all heads of security institutions and members

of parliamentary committees on defence and security. See Thomas Jaye, "Liberia: Parliamentary oversight and lessons learned from internationalized security sector reform", Center for International Cooperation, New York, 2010, http://issat.dcaf.ch/Learn/Resource-Library/Policy-and-Research-Papers/Liberia-Parliamentary-Oversight-and-Lessons-Learned-from-Internationalized-Security-Sector-Reform. The GRC's report was to be released in early 2007. American officials involved in the SSR process rejected the GRC consultations on the grounds that it would take too long to produce a strategy document (Jaye, ibid., p. 8). President Johnson-Sirleaf sent a request to the US government to outsource policy-making for Liberia's national security strategy to the RAND Corporation despite concerns from more than 80 Liberian civil society groups that greater Liberian input was needed. National Defense Research Institute, note 240 above; Jaye, note 276 above, p. 15.

277 The armed groups were arguably the most organized collective Liberian bodies in the country at the time. They continued to hold on to their arms as an insurance policy, and the commanders maintaining control over these groups should have been prudently engaged.

278 There is a laundry list of technical mistakes made by UNMIL: an overly ambitious start date for DDR (the CPA indicated a start 60 days after the signing of the ceasefire), and cantonment sites had not been constructed during this period, nor were UNMIL military personnel fully deployed.

279 Five senior officers from the former AFL were eventually reinstated because the AFL lacked senior leadership to lean on during the reform process.

280 de Vries and van Veen, note 4 above.

281 Ball and Hendrickson, note 32 above; Brzoska, note 32 above.

282 McFate, note 251 above.

283 United Nations, note 2 above, p. 6.

284 Bryden and Scherrer, note 1 above, pp. 6, 12.